Filaments
of
Sentiments

A Collection of Poetry

Robert Rarus

Green Valley Publishing ™

Contents

Filaments of Sentiments

III.   Of the Arts and Culture 33

IV.   Reflections of Spain 47

VII. Of Human Affairs 83

VIII. Of History, Traditions, and Folklore 101

IX.   Of World Affairs and the Commonweal

X.   Humorous Musings

XI.   Of Dreams, Magic, and Mysticism

XII.   Meditations 149

XIII. Of God and Spirituality 169

XIV. Of Old Age and Beyond............181

Prologue

To the Reader:

In you, whoever you are, my book perusing,

I find a grateful audience, for which I am grateful.

On each page, you will find me;

There, I will be waiting for you.

For My Family

I.   Of Childhood

CONSTELLATIONS OF CHILDHOOD

When trouble visits, I think of simpler times,
The days when the morning stars sang together;
There I inhabit the psychic olfactories of yore
Which preserve the sweet aromas of my youth.
In the silver bath of memory,
Faded remote images gradually take shape and emerge—
Sledding down white hibernal hills and building igloos in the snow;
Finding the sure estival green sanctuary of climbing our favorite tree;
Raking rusted autumn leaves and carving jack-o-lanterns;
All of these pure visions crystallize from their quiescence,
As evoking a clear and true note of a musical instrument,
Derived through the correct tension of a well-tuned string;
All are memories joyful and redolent of carefree innocence,
Coupled with the constellations of childhood.
When heart is open, enjoined by mind's eye,
These faint sights and sounds beckon me still,
To travel back to familiar echoes,
Only then to realize, in my desire to return,
It is nothing that wish can conceive,
Nor can felicity bring to pass.

A BOY PLAYED ON THE SEASHORE

A boy played on the seashore where the waves fell,
Diverting himself now and then with his fun—
To find a smoother pebble or a prettier shell,
Along the sea-sands, glistened by sun.

Before him, undiscovered and unfurled,
The great ocean lay vast and beyond;
Content he had discovered the entire world,
On the seashore, the boy played on.

ON WINTRY WINDOWS

On wintry windows the frost designs
Make marvelous magic to the eyes of the child;
A soft-white polygon pattern shines

Through back-lit landscapes of the winter wild,
The silvery stuff of the child's imagination,
While he dreams of days of springtime mild.

He scratches his initials as a secret designation
Of his presence, as he savors the fleeting luminescence,
Denoting with his fingernail his proud demarcation

Of a private moment of simple magnificence.

INDIAN HEAD

If I could just get back to the River,
At the bottom of Green Valley,
Everything would be okay—
Back to that twelve-year-old again,
During days green and carefree,
Back to my childhood idyllic riverside Arcadia,
Traversing that copse of white birches,
Crossing those timeless miniature canyons of feeding runnels and rills,
Navigating the pebbles across those sanctified streams,
Standing beneath the rugged oaks lining those familiar fluvial sandbanks,
Perched beside the silted shallows in the pure serene,
With crude fishing pole in hand,
Casting out from shore just a few short yards,
Happy for whatever fish might be biting.
Back in those days, I spent hours reverential,
Sitting atop that pale red shale promontory,
Atop our dear Indian Head,
With its wild overgrown grizzled grasses, just below the Enfield Dam;
There I used to gaze across the silvery River to the other side,
As though beholding beatific some remote, undiscovered continent.

It's been long since I've called these visions to my eyes;
The River still resides within me;
Too rare, grow now my visits there.

DEAR SEVEN-YEAR-OLD

When I was age seven, ageless ages ago,
I once thought to myself, "Years from now, when I come
To be an adult, I surely won't become
One who believes that children just don't know."

Since that time, often I have met
The travails of adulthood and its abundant sorrows,
Remembering my yesterdays and facing my tomorrows—
Dear Seven-Year-Old: I did not forget.

II.   Of Nature

CELESTIAL ELOQUENCE

1

I am but a humble witness of the evening skies,
As I behold the wonders of the ancient starscape,
The sacred spectra, the glory of the night;
I sing beatific of the immutable galaxies of stars in the firmament,
Eager to come to earthly terms with the distant unattainable.

2

Suffused divine light has thrilled the sight of all beholders,
As illumined mortals raise their eyes in spectacle
To apprehend the radiant rondure of the heavens,
Gazing at arched avenues of stars, with necks craned.
As the lamps of Heaven flicker with a faint, softened light,
Those who enter the divine temple are unwilling to leave it,
With eyes enchanted by the remote altar of the mystical empyrean expanse,
Awestruck by the enormity of the celestial spheres.
The worldly is repulsed afar from that edifice,
Dark canvas of the cosmos, the tenebristic night sky;
The marked majesty of the Milky Way is a sight that all but confounds metaphor,
Rendering articulate voices mute.
I am transported with the fleeing magic of the stars that shoot athwart in the night;
As the heavenly bodies hold their swift, silent course,
At once the centrifugal and centripetal forces sing the communal choral hymn.
We seek the assured constancy of the Cynosure,
Remaining perplexed by ancient questions of primordial provenance,
As Nature's laws still lay hid in the night.

3

Surrounded by the tacit majesty of whispered light,
We feebly toss lassos at the infinite,
Hailing the Architect, sidling alongside the universe,
As if to render recondite mysteries inert.
As with departed human souls, whose past deeds continue to resonate on earth,
Even the light from bygone stars still shines brightly in our eyes.
We behold the many, and we behold each one,
For one star differs from another star in glory;

In humble supplication, we pray that we may be clothed in their singular light.
So faultless a structure, Our Lord has erected;
Whence are we who marvel at the vast heavens,
That which will long outlive us?
Let silence speak like an epiphany star.

ORB

Latent in a bright blue daytime sky
Emerges a pale white moon,
Appearing as an elusive truth manifested,
Faint, yet always in plain sight,
But to have to look.
A subtle orb is peeking out of the obscured obvious,
Still abiding, hiding diurnal,
Omnipresent, yet unseen by most,
Until darkness descends.

ALPINE MEADOWS

During six short-lived weeks of summer
Flourish the fleeting flowers of alpine meadows,
Low-cropped in aspect, bearing soft white blossoms.
They patiently abide their quiescent wait,
Ere they bloom behindhand, born but to smile and fall;
Their kind arrays suddenly adduce sacred Creation itself,
Proudly displayed across the lea with indivisible glory—
Let a thousand thousand flowers shout in shape and color!
Then they quietly slip back into humble dormancy,
Back under the covers, furtively forfeiting their tenuous skeins,
To bloom but ephemeral, with a fugitive farewell,
Yet bequeathing treasured visions of their evanescent poesy,
Emblazoned imprimaturs still alive in loving hearts,
As patient as the saxifrage which persists among the rocks.

SAUNTER

A brown calico cat saunters across a busy road,
As if to invite disaster;
Arriving safely satisfied,
He pounces with lynx eyes upon the moths;
Then unperturbed, he slowly saunters on.

TAIL WAGGING

We used to walk in the early morning,
Casting two long shadows in the twilight, never lagging;
I loved to watch your shadow, with tail wagging.

Your love was absolute, as all pure love is;
You sensed my emotions, like no human ever could;
Your faithful shadow reflected the good.

Now, in early morning, I walk alone,
Casting only my own shadow, spirit sagging;
Missing your shadow, with tail wagging.

THE DOVECOTE

Constrained by a life of quiet ennui,
A morning commuter stops in the quotidian gridlock,
Looking upward in a solitary moment,
To notice a fetching sight for resigned eyes,
As if somehow transformed by fortune.
A flock of white doves flies freely overhead in augury,
A magnificent white mass of truant spirits, moving as one,
In gyre against a sky of pure azure;
Kinetic beauty is laid manifest,
As the flock casts its shifting penumbra on the earth below,
Unfettered and unconstrained, sundered from all restriction,
Yet nonetheless resigned to return to the dovecote,
That unhasped refuge where sustenance and security lie.

GEESE IN FLIGHT

I marveled one evening at the scintillant sight of geese in flight,
A sojourn designed through divine inscrutable instinct,
A flock flying as one in their arcane geometry,
A complex, shifting isosceles vector, as if a proof of Euclid;
It were as though a moving temple in flight,
As bright as a parable concerning birds,
A useful reminder of what men choose to forget.
I heard an avian chorus of hortatory honking,
All urging one another to advance in their airborne parabolic procession,
Manifesting Heaven's holy order, the obverse of chaos and accident.
I was never more certain, in that rapturous moment,
Of His sacred design, an epiphany of theophany,
A wondrous beatitude to behold in the solitary sky.

THE RAM

While hiking in the wilds, along the glacial lakes of Waterton,
High on a wilderness mountaintop,
As remote and lofty as the eagle's aerie,
I saw a bighorn sheep, a large ram,
Emerging furtively from the deep brush,
Manifesting formidable horns,
Horns which might have gotten caught in the thicket
At some indeterminate ancient time.
The ram approached slowly, coming up very close to me,
Tilting its horned head in curiosity,
Regarding me with his odd, rust-colored eyes,
Rare topaz marbles, strange irises speckled with granular wonderment.
I felt as though I ought to be afraid,
Yet somehow I knew that the ram meant me no harm,
And somehow the ram knew that I meant no harm also;
And somehow I sensed how the ram understood all that.
Curiosity satisfied, the ram slowly turned in peace
And quietly walked away, returning to the dense thicket.

BAMBOO FOREST

I am living in a bamboo forest;
The sonic splendor of a windy night is sheer delight.
Hitting harmonic, one against the other,
The stalks all speak in their eloquent dialect,
Performing their exotic percussive symphony.
They all stand resolute, somehow timeless,
As a distant Eastern ink print of a bamboo forest.

WHEN WILL THE ASTER APPEAR?

The chaliced red tulip peeks out in spring,
As the timid crocus emerges,
While the yellow daffodil appears in April;
At that time, the impatient then ask,
When will the aster appear?

White yarrow steps forth in summer,
With pink rose and petaled coneflower,
As the orange tiger-lily abounds in July;
All the while, the impatient still ask,
But when will the aster appear?

Come September, with patience rewarded,
As the leaves betray a faint hint of russet,
The lavender aster finally appears,
Blossoming bright in the autumn dew.
As with human cultivations, the last shall be first:
To bloom belated is to bloom eternal.

III.   Of the Arts and Culture

THE RICHEST FLOWER

We are adjured to consider the artist,
Curiously spellbound by transcendent fancies and allusions,
At once enthralled by the saint and the mystic.
A pure light of God burns within them;
Artists create what they know, what they see,
What at bottom of their hearts they wish for.
Emotion is transmuted into images of mimesis, making mysteries graspable,
Illuminating the simple beauties of everyday life—
The sounds of raindrops on the leaves, the soft light of silvery glistening clouds—
All blessings are enraptured in a sweet and elusive tranquility,
Beckoned by redolent calls from a poesy of hidden sources,
An afflatus affirmed by a return to long-forgotten visions and remote reckonings.
Mills are in movement, gentle in motion,
Articulating the eloquent speech of the heart,
That it never be silenced, for storm nor for wind,
Pervading the world with a wondrous solace;
Revived ardor, the flame for a life wonderful,
Burns incessantly, seeking sublime expression,
Soaring towards the ineffable,
As climbing, clinging vines of a searching wisteria,
Concepts taken in and nurtured, as a foundling or wandering waif.
All of this is defined in concrete forms,
Yet vague and implicit, beguiled by nuances so essential, so elusive to describe,
As to endeavor to express the difference in taste between a pear and an apple.
We are enjoined to surrender to the love of earthly shapes,
Apprehended by charms of color and line,
Bedighted by greens and blues and yellows, together,
Forming a consonant symphony of hue.
We behold the efflorescence of things seen and yet unseen,
Elevated towards the unattainable,
More to be savored than can be known or can be told—
That rare and pure cynosure, raised to the rank of magic and mysteries.
The Richest Flower of beautiful form,
In our garden, so we must cultivate.

THE SKAGEN LIGHT

At the northernmost tip of Jutland lies a small seacoast village;
There the painters flock in pilgrimage,
All seeking a mystical light found nowhere else.
All endeavor to capture that which defies catalogue or constraint,
Favoring things over names for things,
Setting forth wheresoever with pigment and brushes in search of *plein air*,
Celebrating the timeless, grasping the ephemeral.
They pursue the endless light of endless beaches,
Wishing somehow to render reverie inscrutable onto canvas,
Chasing pastel aspects of sunlight, gently suggested,
Mysterious hints of hue borne well into the gloaming.
All are transfixed by the translucence of scintillant sea and sky,
Paying homage to transformations triumphant;
They cherish the ever-changing glow,
Fervently clinging to the fleeting luminescence,
Securing it deep within their innermost hearts,
As one holds precious the evanescent magic of a shooting star.
As pervading silence welcomes the gentle sounds of nature,
So we do not shun the luminous ambiguity;
We rather race toward the marvelous burning uncertainty,
All embracing the simple dignity of doubt and the wisdom of insecurity.

VELÁZQUEZ IN THE MIRROR

Enraptured by luminous essences in chiaroscuro,
Partaking in the beckoning brightness,
Standing well behind the farthingaled figures
Of the ladies in waiting, *las meninas,*
Hidden in the tenebristic background, holding his paintbrush,
The mysterious master appears.
A theologian of painting is revealed obscure in a mirror,
Inhabiting the circumscribed province of genius,
With an admixture of pigment and artistic verisimilitude,
In a masterpiece painted not by hand,
But by the pure force of will.
He smiles, as if to let us in on his secret,
Imparted to those who will notice,
Those who would wink back at him in the canvas.

SHACKLES

Enchanted by a lost alchemy
Of worshiped light and peculiar luminosity,
When I was once in a reddish mood,
I painted a tree in vermilion;
Feeling a bit injured, as it struck me just so,
I painted its curve to the point of deformation;
There and then, my shackles came off.

QUATRAINS

I delight in the quatrains of the ancient Persian poet,
Universal musings of a Sufi mystic bard,
Penned in script of cryptic characters,
Written arcane, from right to left;
Incantations are conveyed by translations of text
Proffered by the Western scholar,
Carefully crafted with poetic art,
Conveying the breathing soul of the poet.
Metrical phrases show a scholarly alchemy,
Far transcending mere linguistic recitation,
As a gifted concert pianist infuses deep emotions
Which can never be captured on a printed sheet of music,
As a master painter coats the canvas with a magic
Far beyond the geometrics of a stolid blueprint drawing.
I absorb these genial verses of the gentle Persian poet,
Speaking to me now across the ages,
An artful articulator of enduring dreams,
With kind offerings wonderfully preserved,
Words which survive the life of mortal men.
I drink these wondrous quatrains on the eve of winter solstice,
As though these ancient lines are blazing logs of light,
All rolling down remote nocturnal hills,
In promise of the bold returning sun,
Illuming the darkness, spinning dervishly.

STILTED

The poem contained an epigraph from Aeschylus—
Inscripted in Greek alphabet, no less!
Displaying use of language smooth as satin—
With phrases set in French, Italian, Latin.

Their wont is to parade obscure allusions—
No matter this creates such stark confusions.
With treasure hunts so stiff and so robotic—
They never speak in terms plain and demotic.

Its brilliance, we concede, that much is true;
Yet we must ask, as so we labor through
The labyrinth of each pedantic hurdle,
Why Brilliance must be wearing such a girdle.

Such verse is crafted as a panegyric
To academic stylists esoteric;
Words penned through veil of shade and stilted view,
Written for an audience of few.

ON PUBLISHING

They're selling validation at the corner store,
Many stand in line for admittance;
They pine for acceptance through a stubborn door,
For to stand outside is "good riddance".

Their walls are adorned with rejection letters—
It's hopeless, they intuit;
But to fear the snickers, as derision unfetters—
That's not a reason not to do it.

THE BUSKERS

1

In the timeless theatrical stage of street,
There plays the perennial symphony, the magical musicale,
Ever so since ancient times;
Witness the buskers, playing with bravura their studied musical craft.
Pursuing elusive artistic dreams,
Deriving penurious sustenance from sustaining others,
Their sweet music falls softer than blown petals in the breeze.
Lords and lasses of the lyre,
Beleaguered, yet unabashed and unbridled,
They apply their learned hands upon their instruments,
As accomplished fingers begin to play,
Commanding the strings to evoke their deepest passions.
Listen to the pleasant longings of guitars and mandolins,
Of accordions and fiddles, flutes and tambourines,
Performing Celtic strains gaily, reminiscent of a lively ceilidh,
Or playing Cajun melodies of long ago, from a *fais-do-do*.

2

Purveyors of rhyme and rhythm, they lend welcome respite
To the stubborn hubbub of daily modern life.
As plying a windlass in a deep well,
With buckets of cool water, they slake many thirsts;
Bystanders are enjoined by their hearts to stop,
Perchance to hear *provençal* strains of the great folkloric diapason,
Counterpoising the surrounding cacophony.
Choristers sing bright roundelays and sweet love ballads,
As medieval troubadours once sung of love.
Songsmiths of madrigals are masterful in devising gallant surprises,
Sung as gently as a chorus of larks and linnets,
Conveyed through sublime voices, harmonic and antiphonal,
With ears attuned to the high silver strains.
As generous sonic apothecaries, they dispense their cures,
All in consonant tension and release,
Resolving to find elemental sweetness and harmony,
Conveying joy through colorful musical conversation,
Kissing the hallowed countenance of their sister sounds.

BEYOND PLAYED INSTRUMENTS

The sum is often greater than the parts;
No truer is this shown than in the arts.
The band heard music strange through their P.A.,
Rare sounds emitted, notes they didn't play;
Defying reason, though it made no sense—
Somehow they all made magic,
Beyond played instruments.

FRETLESS

The musical master plays a fretless instrument,
Applying boundless subtleties, used to augment
The nuances of notes not permitted by a fret,
Producing fine performances beyond the limits set.

Some deem his intentions as an exercise laborious,
A futile act of hubris, pointless and vainglorious;
And so it is, with the pure of heart, whose actions will beget
False judgments levied at their feet, as they play without a fret.

THE DRUMMER

Strike the kettle drums, thunder the tympany,
Tap the congas, bang the timbales, thrum the tabor;
Hear the extrusions of ringing crashes and muted beats.
Hit the snare drum, proclaim it loudly,
Then caress it softly with a gentle roll.
All is punctuated by a conversation held in syncopated rhythm;
Now listen to the drummer speak.

COLTRANE

Some stories must be told without words,
In a language that makes the most sense in the end.
Its eloquent spokesman speaks to us now—
Man, you should hear this cat play!
Evincing and evoking, combining the raw with the gentle,
Blending the screaming with the subtle,
The sentient with the primal,
He is the high priest of hieratic scales,
The better craftsman who puts his arms around the world
Through his living breath.
He performs with ambling embellishments,
Given to rhapsodic riffs and dithyrambic exaltations;
The silent spaces are as precious as the playcd notes.
Plying the bounce of the bebop, serving as the soul's backstop,
Such a musical polyglot regales us still;
His vocabulary is tireless, of breathless skill,
His timeless tone immutably pure;
His melodies are distant, yet somehow familiar and near,
As though to wish us happy birthday.

STEP LIGHTLY

Step lightly, the jazzman once decreed,
Through sentences spoken with piano keys,
As subtle as the softest breeze,
Articulated footsteps, light indeed,
As is done here.

ESOTERIC APPLAUSE

The symphony violinist gently taps her bow on the music stand,
While another softly rubs her sheet music with her bow's edge,
In quite acknowledgment of the brilliant soloist;
The entire orchestra quietly shuffles its feet,
In decorous communal recognition.

The rock drummer clicks together his drumsticks with alacrity,
As an affectionate nod to his bandmates onstage.
At the billiards tournament, the thumping of cue sticks on the floor
Celebrates a wondrous bank shot, in sonic imprimatur.
The hockey players all clack their sticks on the ice in unison,
In tribalistic tribute to honor one of their own.
It is true, they all do peculiar things;
Beneath these arcane customs lies a strange solidarity,
A distinctive commonality shown in collective tacit joy:
Such is the subtle beauty of esoteric applause.

THE RADIO BASEBALL ACCOUNT

"Don't look for a pitch you can't hit",
Advises the old veteran in the booth.

Listen to the curious poetry of the radio baseball account,
Capturing that certain comfort of the daily rhythms of the game;
The soothing voice frames the picture on a pitch-black slate,
Anchoring me as I careen alone down somnolent dark roads,
Hurtling through the pervading night.
Hear the pauses for effect, rendered with license for hyperbole;
The announcer confects stark kinetic images,
Against the crack of the bat and the occasional roar,
Against the constant hubbub of the crowd.
Yes, I am certainly there,
Beckoned by the hypnotic, lyrical voice,
Guiding me until I arrive safely home.

I AM CLEMENTE

1

A Caribbean jewel hails fresh from his native island;
He becomes a catapulted champion.
"Let's go!", *Arriba!*—the fans all chant in unison;
This performance bears no *libretto*, no script;

Here all the action is spontaneous, surprising, poetic.
He is a graceful ballet dancer,
Elegantly moving in *chassés, sautés*, and *glissades*;
See his gracile figure run, jump, and glide in kinetic beauty!
The artist's tools are gloves made of leather
And beveled bats made of ash.
The crowd buzzes as he plays with relentless skill,
And with unreserved abandon;
He approaches each play as if it might be his very last.
At bat, he swings from his heels, in late-inning heroics;
In the field, with singular graceful carriage,
He makes the great plays look easy;
He throws them out from right field with his cannon arm.

2

He plays with contagious passion, adding no little fuel—
That sort of humorous byplay between men under pressure,
Marked by genial satire, wholly convivial.
He refuses to change his jersey while on a winning streak;
He is often overlooked and misunderstood in a strange land;
He quietly amazes from the obscure side of the color line.
His flatterers compare him to Mays;
Indignant, he exclaims: "I am not Mays. I am Clemente."

3

His final act of life is in service to others;
"I am from the poor people."
After the crash at sea, thousands flock to the shore,
To be nearby the place where his plane went down.
Someone can be heard, in a makeshift Spanish elegy:
"Roberto está por ahí en alguna parte—
Él todavía está aquí."
"Roberto is out there somewhere—
He is still here."

OPEN THE DOOR QUICKLY

1

From the Renaissance to the Impressionists,
So much has vanished in the mists;
From the fine baroque to the Byzantine,
Art suffers when it isn't seen.

Open the door quickly, for we are lost.
What hidden artistic treasures lie silently sleeping,
Relegated to distant, dimmed pyres and forgotten obsequies?
How many masterpieces are never to grace museum walls?
How many plays written, symphonies composed,
Never to regale an unwitting audience?
Would that timeless words might reach our ears,
Only to be written in the wind and running water,
Penned by those whose names lie dark,
But whose transmitted brilliance will never die.
Indeed they reside inviolable among us still,
As flowers to bloom unseen in the wilderness,
Numberless like hovering dreams,
Those who humbly pray that their lamps at midnight
Might be seen in some high lonely tower.

2

Enter the curators and impresarios of banality,
Those who brush aside artistic masters
As though they were mere mosquitoes.
They oust beauty in deference to crass exhibitions and boring absurdities.
They promote mindless music that marches madly
To the metronomic hammers of hackneyed hortators.
They are wont to publish worthless opuses of soilure,
Daft, insipid tomes of jejune drivel,
Culminating in a fire of straw, like proverbs gone wrong.
They would ignore the blessed poetic ink which fell from Shakespeare's pen,
All the while extolling the sad detritus of dunces.
The consonance of their dissonance is on display,
Caught in the sordid pastimes of exhausted minds;
The depths of their nature are not easily sounded.

Dumbfounded spectators all gaze in studied wonderment,
Constrained to behold a febrile culture in free-fall,
Carrying within itself the seeds of its own decay.

Open the door quickly; we must be gone, or we are lost.

ARACHNE[1]

An audacious mortal once had the temerity
To challenge Athena to a contest of the arts;
And so they matched their highest dexterity,
Tapping deeply from the dcpths of their hearts.

Arachne confected her finest weaving,
Her tapestry woven of rich silk threads;
Hcr beautiful work was beyond believing—
Golds and silvers, blues, greens, and reds.

As Athena could find no fault as decider,
Hence she rebuked her rival in ire;
She cursed Arachne to become a spider—
Metamorphosis was her punishment dire.

And so it is with Jealousy's doings,
Such artists who lay their intentions bare;
Consigning their rivals to gossamer ruin,
Setting their countenance in a stare.

---

[1] See Ovid, *Metamorphoses*

IV.   Reflections of Spain

THE AQUEDUCT OF SEGOVIA

Stretching high into the Spanish sky,
Bold gray granite arches span the countryside,
Redolent of their faded Roman architects;
Our eyes follow their straight line to the vanishing point.
Once long ago, at an imperceptible angle of pitch, coaxing gravity,
Their flumes conveyed water from remote hinterlands,
Flowing through uncastled provinces,
In quiet answer to long-vanished supplications of an ancient city's denizens.
All which remains is this mysterious stone testament;
The solution of the mystery is the moral of the story.

ÁVILA

Somewhere on a vast Iberian plain,
Poetically pitched above the gentle verdant escarpment,
A medieval walled city majestically appears,
Constructed with ancient stones of tans and muted reds,
Intertinged with faint strains of pale green lichens.
There pilgrims are still enjoined to pay homage
At the simple home of a humble native saint;
The city quietly keeps watch as faithful sentinel,
Peering through the weathered, crenellated walls,
Smiling knowingly.

FROM A SPANISH MEDIEVAL VILLAGE

The women are scrubbing their laundry together,
In a common stone basin for this simple chore;
Their medieval village is untouched by time,
Bound by traditions of history and lore.

They drown humble garments once worn by their forbears,
Living in beautiful, time-honored ways;
The men return from their toil in the orchards,
Harvesting as if in the time of Cervantes.

49

We overhear in foreign tongue
The timeless truths which must be sung,
As durable as their ancient foundry;
The women continue to scrub their laundry.

EL RUSO PAVLOV

I read about *El Ruso Pavlov*,
In a way so strange to my eyes;
A random tome on a Spanish bookshelf,
Curiosity met my surprise.

Ideas well-acquainted, yet unique,
In a manner not easily won;
And for native eyes to see this as familiar—
I could easily see this done.

LIBERTAD

A stranger approached me,
Direct and unabashed;
I was somewhat nonplussed—
"Qué quieres?", I asked.

He summoned his thoughts,
It was just a bid odd;
His reply was most simple:
"Quiero Libertad." [2]

---

[2] "What do you want?"; "I want liberty."

THE POPPY FIELDS OF TOLEDO

Outside a Spanish medieval city,
Sprawling fields of wild scarlet poppies appear;
Their bold colors shine as rare geodes.
They lie at odds with the gray pallid portraits
Painted by *el hijo favorito*[3] of the town;
Would that El Greco had painted these bright red poppies!

---

[3] the favorite son

V.   Sketches of an Island

SKETCHES OF AN ISLAND

1

When I was weary and would fain get some rest,
I departed with alacrity from the other side,
Mussed and nonplussed with rebarbative banalities,
Scorning the tumults of the city,
Searching after every green thing.
I arrive seeking refuge from denatured life forsworn,
Escaping to a timeless sanctuary of stillness,
Where healing is dispensed through beauty manifold and manifest.
I am apprehended by a magical world which conduces to my happiness,
Where welcome sounds supplant the noxious noises of modernity,
Where birdsongs and breezes melt frowns, weaving sorrows into gilded crowns.
I venture forth immersed in Nature's kind ataraxia,
Regaled by the crashing roar of ocean waves,
And by the constancy of their echoes, quiet and deafening at once,
Engendering a peaceful trance of multiplied reverie.
I am here now, transported with delight,
Amidst layers of atmosphere of sky and sea,
Happily transformed by the peace of the leaping air.

2

By what strange magic is this light so diffused?
By what fortune do I behold such huge, clouded skies,
As those Constable loved to paint?
Bold streaks extend across the pleasant courts of heaven,
Marked white against the sprawling azure, ever commodious and tall.
I see flocks of hundreds of birds, all flying gracefully in wondrous kinetic ways,
A dark mass shifting in direction, as one.
I gaze at them long and longingly,
Yearning for the feeling when I first saw them in flight,
Each one of billions equaling the sun's course,
Where curving ocean surrounds the world.
I bide the quiet afternoon hours, surveying the marvelous scintillant expanse
Whence back-lit orange clouds at sunset stand against the proud blue firmament;
Pastel shades of fading sunlight, fugues of fugitive colors,
Reside above white-capped seas of contrasting tourmaline and cobalt blue,
That mysterious watery province which bears the mickle beasts of the ocean.

55

3

The glimmering landscape falls into the gentle eventide.
Now goes the sun under the wood; longing has lighted on me.
Upon descension of the pure naked Night, ascending into celestial magic,
I am surrounded by tenebristic skies,
The quiet dark magnificence filled with heavenly lamps,
As thousands of stars scatter their astral silvery dew, sighing immaculate.
I capture momentary visions of furtive shooting stars,
Flashing and gone athwart the widening welkin,
Luminous crumbs which fall from the festal board on high.
A nearby beach fire, perhaps a votive offering,
Sends bright sparks ascending in gyre into the night sky,
Whirling as gamboge mothlike spirits, surrounded by soft-lit countenances.
Listen to the grating roar of countless seaside pebbles,
Worn rocks which the waves draw back and then fling upon the shore,
Patiently repeating in eternal steady cadence,
That playful timeless plashing of the tidal ebb and flow.
The lighthouse emits into darkness its transient, pale-green, diaphanous light,
An ephemeral speck of luminosity gamboling, searching,
Searching for witnesses scattered through the boundless night,
Pervading the sea with prophetical light;
The mystic moonlight dances on the dark ocean tides.

4

The estival evening fireflies flit in their random cavalcades,
Tiny flambeaus in flight, with scattered, flickered flashes,
Emitting their wonderfully-strange, short-lived incandescence.
Spirits fill the air with nocturnal cricket-music,
All performed amidst beckoning shadows, moving in mystical play,
As though animated and breathing, lost in the illusion of a grateful game.
As the sea's many voices permeate the night,
I traverse the mysterious moon-blanched beaches,
Scarcely discerning great sable silhouettes beyond the grassy dunes,
Amidst the dense growth of salty briar roses, their aroma sweet.
I absorb the peace of timeless days, sustaining into evening's sweet repose,
Pleasantly deafened by an evensong chorus of nightingales,
Sung with cheerful good-night air,
In a silence and solitude not easily found elsewhere;
I slowly drift off to sleep, dreaming of marvels which somehow remain.

5

Ere Heaven's fairest light, greeted by the eyelids of the morning,
Incessant roars of surf pervade the air.
After daybreak, I stroll the shore, pausing to hear premonitory distant thunder,
As dark storm clouds quickly scud across the sky,
Ominous, yet somehow beautiful.
Fleeting portentous lightning flashes precede fulminating thunderclaps,
Exclamations in bold, magnificent commotion,
Tympanic against the strange colloquy of wind and rain.
I become enamored of salty breezes,
Enchanted with the steady soughing of wild winds;
I seek treeline shelter in a grove of shadbushes,
Under their pendulous branches outstretched overhead.
Behold the peaceful entropy of a raging storm!
Rough waves soon foam white and welter, crashing wildly on the shore;
Beneath the unsettled empyrean expanse, amidst elusive mists of gray,
The torrent slowly subsides, marked by the iridescent aerial bow.

6

The great winds blow shoreward, as the salt tides flow seaward;
Ocean forces present indomitable.
The sea and wind are in constant movement;
The waves follow one after another, prolific in their eternal pursuit,
In the froth and drift of the sea.
I am immersed in a dream unfathomable,
A trance intractable, a reverie ineluctable;
I absorb mythic wonders well beyond my wildest esperance.
A litany of surging whitecaps approaches,
Untamed, undulating, bubbling, gurgling, careering, crashing,
Subsiding, subsumed, spuming, reconstituting, repeating,
Over and over, fold-by-fold.
As Truth, the surf does not hurry, nor does it tarry,
All in a mystical rhythm of its own.
It serves no clock; it is the clock itself.

Scattered raindrops alight on me, as gentle aspersions of holy water,
As though sacramentally dispensed, somehow remotely baptismal.
I hear plaintive cries of returning gulls,
Suggestive of the intonations of enrobed muzzeins,

Calling out for prayer from elevated minarets.
A distant foghorn emotes a bold, deep tone,
Perchance a sonic evocation of the blowing of a shofar.
I hear the thrumming of steady, stubborn gales, blind and instinctual,
As though faint ragas summoning the enigmatic murmurs of mystics.
The melodious winds suspire strange utterances,
Akin to the arcane musical strains of Aeolian harps,
Encouraged by the desultory currents of warbling breezes.
Together, all of these sweet voices conjoin in curious harmonic serendipity.
I am blessed by all the voices; they all welcome me here.

7

The zephyrs continue to play gently.
I wend my way along the shore, pacing the resounding sea-beach,
Happily traversing expanses of ribbed sand.
I see a fresh array of storm-strewn shells—
The symmetrical spirals of whelks and the fine brown lines of cockles,
All displaying Nature's perfect geometry.
Behold the simple elegance of the quahog,
Humble gray mollusks ensconced along the shore.
All are bejeweled amulets, somehow sanctified.
In the shallows, the limpid waters are as fine crystal;
Below the tideline, a magical mirror appears on the wet dun sand,
That smooth intercession between sea and land.
As the steady surf effaces my footprints,
I submit to the gentle sensation of my feet sinking slowly in the soft mud,
Happily embedded, wondrously tactile.
I plunge into the water, immersed and submerged, awash in the brine,
Swimming out beyond the white seafoam,
Then conveyed by the gliding waves to shore.
All the while, tidal pools pullulate with sea life—
Delicate algae, sea anemones, crabs, starfish, and slipper snails;
Prehistoric horseshoe crabs bear their crude brown shells,
As medieval cuirasses of protection, as antique suits of armor.
Sandpipers, ruffs and reeves, dart along the moving tideline,
As doughty seagulls stroll the beach.
Makeshift sculptures of rock cairns dot the shore,
Tenuous constructions, hardly foursquare.
I am given to adventitious wanderings in the great tidal expanse,
Stumbling upon a spiritual morphology, unique and perpetual.

8

I see young children playing on the beach and in the water.
They construct their castles with saltwater moats, fleeting donjons of sand;
They are kindly redolent of healing joy, of simple play and unfettered fun,
Evocative of my own childhood.
In their pure exuberance, they display a world of perfect innocence,
Bearing the unconscious wisdom that frolic is far from frivolous;
They are unwitting masters of the practiced art of detachment,
Welcome accelerants to higher places of spirit.
I bear witness to all of them, praying that I may never become so erudite
As to become unwise.

That selfsame day, I spend long afternoon hours lying quietly in the sun,
Accessing that most rare of places, where time is completely blotted out.
Evening descends, and again I find slumber,
Thinking of the day's visions, bespeaking bales of happiness,
Suggesting sanctuary.

9

I awake to gentle birdsongs, arising the next morning,
Not yet knowing of the day's magic which might betide.
I beguile my morning hours in a peaceful traverse through silken mists;
Here a gentle walk provides more simple answers
Than all the tomes of metaphysics.
I partake in a loving fulfillment of premonitory dreams,
Strolling through pleasant bowered paths of shade where the cricket sings,
With spiraling vines twisting and aspiring heavenward.
I walk through venerable groves of shadbushes,
With their great gnarled trunks and branches outstretched,
As bold arms of supplication against the sky,
All in their unmatched elegant mystery.
As their silhouettes rise like black ink prints,
Frisky squirrels dart along their topmost branches.
Going farther afield into long, green dales,
I am environed by sunshine and shade, birds and flowers,
With the scent of hawthorn blowing 'round;
The salt wind blows the feather out of my cap,
And so I stick a violet there to replace it,
Breathing a silent thanksgiving to God.

10

I am surrounded by crowning mercies in rare light,
All vouchsafed by heaven, landscapes arrayed in painterly deployments,
As a flourishing garden of promised delights, natural triumphs,
Magnificent and lavish, yet simple.
The days here are as fleeting as ephemeral vernal ponds,
All defying adequate description;
I am clearly lost in a preponderance of wonder,
Pausing to consider the lilies of Elysian fields.
I am carefully attuned to the merging multitudes of tiny scents and sounds;
I glide across green meadows, roaming through kind expanses of sward,
Through mossy ways lined with lush bracken ferns,
Crowned by masses of unwontedly fine flowers.
Each blossom is an unfolding miracle,
An assemblage of refulgent anadems and diadems—
The gold-dusted yellows of wild mullein and cinquefoil,
Of buttercups, snapdragons, and goldenrod,
Bespeckled by the white-knit tapestries of Queen Ann's Lace.
I embrace the laughing efflorescence of spectral lavenders,
Of lupines, larkspurs, wild chicory, and asters, along with pink thistle,
All the plantings of angels, all breathing together in the humble grass,
All wonderfully fragrant withal—
Behold the magical elegance of these wildflowers!
How could such sweet hours be reckoned, but with their abundant grace?
Bees busily flit among the floral blossoms,
While a fine reticulated spider web appears, with fresh droplets of dew,
Shining softly on the white gossamer.
I remember to prize the small as well as the great;
What moves in the minute world of the grasses, I hold dear.
I see a gliding palette of orange, dozens of monarch butterflies,
Denizens of a world diurnal, bright inhabitants of the air,
With soft little fluttering wing-beats, alighting in yellow fields of goldenrod;
Several of these souls in flight accompany me,
Perhaps as spirit guides to steward me along my path.

11

Erelong many singing birds appear from the isolation of sky,
As assembly of fine fowls arriving through azure circles,

As though the winds had sprinkled their spirits from various distant directions,
As travelers unknown to one another,
Whom chance has brought together in a carriage.
Pure contralto melodies pervade the air,
Emanating from the embouchures of larks;
Hear the sweet music of these feathered choristers!
Witness the coalescence of this divine congeries—
Cardinals, blackbirds, starlings, swifts, and swallows,
Sparrows, warblers, wrens, finches, and thrush—
All sounding together in unison, whistling their spontaneous cries,
Proclaiming their tranquil coda, loquacious melodists in flight,
With a singular avian rhetoric, all speaking their inscrutable language,
Yet plainly apprehended by all of them.
They sing with the simple natural wisdom,
That all of Nature's sounds are somehow music;
They answer and provoke each other's song,
All proclaimed with full-throated ease,
All proclaiming where the senses and passions meet;
Some speak the names we call them by.
Each sits on its perch, as to go through a variety of dreams,
Suggestive of hidden stores and secrct refuges.
All project with bravura in song, in a makeshift composed choir,
Somehow harmonic and antiphonal,
Magical cantatas no human voice could hope to emulate,
In such scale and melody as to cause speech and reason to stand mute;
They all resound in the tilth of God's green garden.
I treasure the portents of augural birds,
Possessing each their ready eloquence, each allaying my discord;
I seek solace as do the migrating birds in the fall,
Steeped in their steady pursuits and habits.
When shall I become as unfettered as the swallow?

12

I reach the other side of the meadow;
Wild grasses and sedges abound in the wetlands.
I see a pristine pond of halcyon, filled with green water lilies,
All flourishing with their white blossoms afloat,
As Monet loved to paint, in especial in old age.

Wind shadows run across the pond;
A pair of snowy egrets stands in the shallows,
Each bearing a fine white feathered coat,
As though constructed of cambric or crinoline;
They wait patiently, silently, stealthily, stilly,
For passing small fishes, as is their wont, to derive their sustenance.
I espy a timorous great blue heron,
Arrayed in its splendid surcotte of tufted cerulean feathers,
Wading slowly through the silvery marshy waters;
Suddenly startled, it departs majestic, gracile and graceful in perfect flight.
The scent of wild grapes pervades the air;
I happen upon a small herd of deer,
Crepuscular creatures feeding through the gloaming;
My steps are marked in the dusk by dim moonlight.
I return to find my rest for the evening,
Soon lost in surrender to the province of dreams,
Fading into slumber amidst the faint cries of owlets
And sweet rustlings of the night-winds,
Immersed in a peace more silent than silence itself.

13

Faint wraiths of morning mist arise slowly, thence into beauty,
And so I awaken.
I walk past quiet farmlands, amidst the gentle tones of lowing cows,
The felicitous stuff of pastoral eclogues.
I greet the rustic countryside and its rolling green pastures,
Its landscape pieced into varicolored patches,
Lined by softly-lit ancient gray stone walls,
Environed by their timeless array of blooms.
All of this possesses the colors of a fairy story,
Evocative of Gaelic legend, of a Druidic dream,
As though summoning the faint strains of uilleann pipes.
There are fields of hay amidst fibers of rye,
Tapestries intertinged with dusky greens and pale browns,
All interstitially woven in wondrous form, all seemingly random,
Yet somehow balanced and ordained.

I then approach the coastline once again,
Walking past fan-like alluvial sediments and huge glacial boulders.
The majestic layered escarpment rises high above the crashing sea below;

The ascending sea-mist wafts into the expanse of blue sky.
The bluffs are bold, yet yielding to erosion,
Tenuous lineaments in tabescent struggle for survival;
The cliffs are steep, yet hardly insuperable.
Here are sundered layers of steady evanescence,
Nature's harsh and lovely architecture, seeking anchors in a world mutable,
Clinging to balance the opposing forces of chaos and constancy,
Of order and entropy.
See the array of countless colors—
Burnt umber, yellow ochre, raw sienna, chalks of white and clays of gray—
Plus multitudes of earth tones and shades, each bearing no appellation,
Hues for which names have yet to be invented.
Marvelous shapes of clay appear,
As though a configured shrine sitting atop a remote promontory;
Here are earthen sculptures borne of raw magnificence,
All formed without chisels, without sculptor's proofs or casts,
All created through patient time by the Ancient of Days.
Hear the reverberations of the raging, pounding surf,
Fostering arcane hypnotic states through their echoes,
Inducing the beckoning trances of magnetic daydreams,
The pull of which remains as strong as the tides.
Breathless, I ply the upward path to the heath,
Passing through diverse ascending layers of bayberry and scrub pine,
Imbued with the scent of salt and evergreen;
Once I reach the top, several fluttering pheasants emerge from the covert.

Late summer light makes its elegant escape into the serenity beautiful;
As daylight once again accedes to night, I peacefully inherit my recollections,
Immersed in such a habitat wholly conceived,
Fortunate enough to reach the fruitful realms;
How perfect is the calm!

14

A dream, a flash of lightning, and a cloud;
Something is removing the ocean's roar from my ears.
It is my last day here.

I must now depart this place of mystic delight,
A structure unique under heaven,
Sacred environs to set artists to dreaming;
Here lie wondrous things which defy comprehension,
The holy hieroglyphics of Nature's beauty.
In this magical terraqueous sphere,
We are avowed to brook the challenge
To protect what has been vouchsafed by heaven,
Unsearchable, marvelous things without number,
A sanctuary that never ceases to render wonder,
Until the stones float upon the sea,
And the trees forbear to sprout in the springtide.

I wend my way through the New England seaside town,
Passing the corollary magnificences of *fin-de-siècle* architecture.
I leave with beatific treasures of cherished remembrances,
Lightfast visions indelibly stamped into the substrate of my mind's eye;
For everything that I did see, did with me talk.
Would that my tongue could utter all the feelings that now arise in me,
Departing a place where the song sings itself, beyond a muffled world.
In the slow accretion of rivulets of experience,
Here I see God in every object, I hear Him in every sound,
Absorbing the manifold aspects of Nature,
Each bearing its unique proprietary structure,
Each possessing a spirit unduplicated, a soul inviolable.

Today is my joy now, and hence forever.
May my shadow be blessed to be cast here again,
Where I leave a good half of my heart,
In a realm affixed and affianced to Heaven.
To this place, nothing can be added;
From this place, nothing can be subtracted.

VI.   Of Human Characters

OF AN ECCENTRIC

There is sound stuff deftly hidden somewhere in the soul of an eccentric,
One who is propelled by sheer will, and by a half a gale of wind.
He is learned, if a little pedantic,
But his prudence is never sacrificed for ostentation;
He highly prizes his capricious collections of curios and oddments.
A blithe paladin of proverbs, he is conscious of the populated mainstream,
But in the main sharply distinct from it;
He is wont to wield a sharp tongue with dullards,
With amused contempt for naïve enthusiasm;
A captive of notions chimerical, he spends his time calculating his net mirth;
In little things, he has sufficiency.
He bears the simple wisdom that words are but a distant approximation.
Preferring the solid to the ephemeral,
He is raffish recipient of raillery for his raiment,
Resolute to maintain his ragged bohemian trappings.
Strolling to the measured meter of life's strange prosody,
He is comfortable in kinship alongside realfolk, artists, and gypsies.
He hazards to use replies pithy and epigrammatic
To those who sit in smug juridical poses,
Deflecting the mockery of the vain and intransigent with lithe ripostes,
While quietly conducting embassies of compliment,
Instilling the incipient murmur of restless hearts.
He ignores the misguided assizes of the banal
Who keep innumerable ledgers with meticulous accuracy;
Verbum sat, a word is enough.
Adept at Homer's craft,
He is a Grub-Streeter whose work remains arcane and unnoticed,
(His eloquence miscast as doggerel),
Conferred with the precarious immortality of a footnote;
As night follows day, the last shall be first.

ODE TO A NARCISSIST

1

How dost thou love thee?
We cannot count the ways.

Enter the narcissist, of haughty mien,
The prince of popinjays and the king of coxcombs,
Amorous of self-bestowed sobriquets;
Drawn to mirrors and to the drone of his own voice,
He is author and orator of his own panegyric.
Given to fustian oratory and stentorian pronouncements,
He knows not the value of omission;
He is a self-appointed oracle who never ceases to oraculate,
Smugly foredooming the aspirations of others;
Hail to a man who knows everything
And always talks about it.
Consigned to vainglorious paths to perdition,
His platitudes are proverbs of ashes;
He is not one of Fortune's favorites.
He insists on showing you a shortcut
And gets lost;
He serenades his sweetheart
When she is ill of a fever.

2

A rascal of irascible temperament,
He is the frequent author of execrable remarks,
Officiously made at the expense of others;
Conveying purported altruistic concerns,
He affects to be kind, while inflicting harm.
He is wont to impart untoward motives to others,
Reflecting his own untoward motives,
Reflecting his own untoward soul, so vast and uninhabited;
He is regaled by the sad misfortunes of others.
He is so easily offended, and yet he so easily offends;
He exhibits the rare and dubious talent of incensing the equable.
He effortlessly insults others,
Then calls them thin-skinned when they are offended,

Responding to their umbrage with persiflage.
Vain and voluble, the most fabulous of fabulists,
He is narrator of fictive accounts of his exploits,
Extolling legends of his factitious deeds.

3

More than a bit solipsistic, he is a bright sun in his personal solar system.
He proudly wears epaulets of self-congratulation,
As a parading, particolored peacock,
As a carpet knight who boasts of his imaginary adventures.
He is a self-canonized patron saint of the sanctimonious,
Pontificating like some highfalutin Rasputin;
Fond of orotund oration,
He is enchanted to refer to himself in the third person;
He prates on with daft mendacities as a dog micturates on a hydrant.
At table he is a querulous whiner and diner,
Bumptious while partaking of the scrumptious;
Prolixity is his propensity,
Given to tedious, turbid monologues, otiose and verbose.
Strutting the magnificence of his pompous wardrobe,
He is consumed with ostentations and frippery.
He liberally volunteers the generosity of others,
And then claims all the credit;
He solicits the ideas of others,
And then claims false authorship for himself.

4

Loathing to be ignored, he consumes attention like laudanum;
When he is rendered invisible, his puerile tantrums are risible.
He cannot abide another commanding the stage,
Flouncing in frustration and annoyance,
Evincing his disdain with ill-mannered harrumphs,
For no stage he occupies is big enough to hold another for long;
He will never forfeit the pulpit.
He thirsts for an audience of fervent adulation;
His practiced flatterers felicitate him;
With baton in hand, he conducts a symphony of sycophants,
All engaged in an interminable war of compliments,
All entranced in their travesties of treacle.

He is disposed to paternalistic trysts,
Displaying impudence in prurience, while capacious in the salacious;
Rife with warped romantic pursuits,
He is choleric and domineering, like Leda's vain swan,
Like a churlish chanticleer.

5

He aspires to be immortalized by sculptured image,
As though through the totems of Tlingits;
He composes his own epitaph that is ten tombstones long.
He languishes in well-merited obscurity,
So indissolubly wed to himself,
Till death would they part.

No narcissist ever thought himself so.

A BRILLIANT MIND

Behold the limitations of a brilliant mind,
The sad circumscriptions that you'll find;
Foolishness, coupled with high erudition,
Is like a perfect engine with a broken transmission;
A mannequin bedecked with fine habiliments
Is raw intelligence without common sense.

He wouldn't hear of reason, this he'd refuse;
Of his fanciful beliefs, they couldn't disabuse.
No matter, all the sage advice they gave him,
In the end, from himself, they couldn't save him.
The sole vestige that remained of his most unyielding mood
Was an unavailing life preserver, floating and eschewed.

DIAGNOSIS

"Patient presents intoxicated",
The diagnosis read;
Consumption had been sated;
The case of beer was dead.

He said that things were all okay,
His words did truly haunt;
I still can hear his voice today:
"I can stop whenever I want."

WHISTLEBLOWER

He stands alone, he scowls at a throne,
He won't atone,
'Cause he knows that he's right;
He holds the sun in his hand, he lights a dark land,
Though he's only one man,
He brings daylight to the night.

He's a dreamful wanderer in sleepless nights,
He continues the fight,
Though he feels the dread;
He's one part saint, he's one part sinner,
He's a saint who says,
"Take this damn halo off my head."

THE HEALER

There is something enlightened afoot here.

As a stone mason patiently repairs a cracked wall,
So proceeds the poet-physician,
The master healer who restores us to good health.
He is charitable as one who rescues the abandoned,

As untiring as one who unblocks channels and rivers to the sea.
His learned intentions are as pure as the elements—
Wind, fire, earth, and water.
His touch is welcome, decisive yet gentle,
As that of a gypsy provoking that crude yet wonderful yawp
Of a raspy chord struck on his weatherbeaten violin.
He conquers maladies through coaxing us
To release from sickness through simple surrender.
He is an able apothecary who dispenses abundant medicines,
Beneficial elixirs derived from leaf, bark, root, and herbs,
Kind heal-all prescriptions from the East,
As though to extract honey from the lion.
He cures with remedies arcane yet salubrious,
As though reuniting human figures with their lost shadows;
Facile it is for him to identify the source of an illness,
As an expert angler may easily locate the fish.
He harnesses healing well beyond treatment of mere symptoms,
Curing the root in order to cure the tree.
Many view the world through a myopic lens of smug, unquestioned conventions;
They fail to comprehend, and so they resort to mocking the healer,
Falsely portraying him as a befeathered voodoo doctor
With a satchel of *gris-gris* by his side.
They so deride as they secretly repair to digging their wells,
Only after they suddenly realize that they have become thirsty.

THE PIONEER

Let us bear witness to those who were anachronisms in their own day.
The work of the pioneer is by its nature imperfect;
So facile, it is, to criticize what was left undone;
Borne of those ideas so obvious,
Once someone else thought of it.
The pioneer upends the granite bedrock of the estates,
Shining a bright beacon of apotheosis into darkness,
An effulgence of the realm,
A long-awaited, illuminated contrast,
A welcome chiaroscuro.

LONELY SOUL

Lonely soul crossing the street at midnight,
Plodding to make it to the other side;
One step, two steps, ever so slowly,
Your silhouette moves along the dotted line.

The traffic light changes, the silhouette fades,
The glaring beams blaze as you move passingly by.
Who will remember your strange, short journey?
The glaring beams fade as you pass shadowy by.

But a moment, but an action,
Insignificant, unrecorded;
Every crosswalk dot a milestone,
Ever so slowly, they pass by.

TRANSISTOR

The road was bespeckled with neon motels, exuding kitsch,
When I got a phone call to receive the news;
And I never quite knew what lonely meant,
Until I heard that he who had lived alone,
Died alone on the night of a blizzard.
Then I recalled vague visions of him,
Long ago, back when he was a teenager,
Holding his transistor radio to his ear.

TOUGH-GUY MYSTIC

A thousand standard deviations from here,
There is a sorry soul, at once serious and comic,
Burning incense in an apoplectic fit,
Championing the signal triumphs of dubious distinction,
Coming across like some fervent, beribboned tough-guy mystic.

Of mauve temperament, he exploits an occult wisdom of the East,
Speaking in silvery sentences of sophistry,
Ushering in a vogue of quaintly-garbed, would-be mahatmas and yogis,
Apprentice sorcerers who regard him with an austere reverence,
As though baring their heads to the playing of the *Marseillaise.*
His lips move indistinctly in cabalistic curses and querulous caterwauls,
With a choleric glare as piercing as a shrill soprano in an off-key choir;
Embracing performative umbrage and outrage,
He fans the flames of fanatics, loathing longanimity;
He is relentless and cannot be doused.

SOMETIMES AN ANGEL

She sheds the endless, long-held conventions;
Not costly her habit, she glides lissome and blithely
Through the immutable permutations of pulchritude.
She walks in beauty in sweatpants;
Sometimes and angel walks in Converse All-Stars.

VISCOUNTS

They aspire to seek congress
With the meek who would abide them;
They are at once charming and devious,
Animated by alternate faces
Of paper smiles and cross gesticulations,
Strutting imperious like vain viscounts.
They twist themselves into pernicious contortions,
As cruel kestrels, smug falcons
Who seek to solidify their sorry abuse;
But absent a compliant quail,
They are powerless and lost in their vile falconry.

THE MUSIC MAN

She kissed the music man as she walked by,
Bright like the morning star, unseen and as yet ungrasped;
Her ephemeral kiss was somehow absolute,
In the rare grace of the moment.
Then she cast a provisional goodbye,
Timid by calculation,
Cheering his troubadour countenance,
As he endeavored to return the magic,
Singing with a hundred evidences of his warmth,
With love transposed in another key.

THE WALKER

Instilled with penetrating, resolute eyes,
He ambles the roadside every day,
A local fixture as fixed as the town green;
His gait is steady, purposeful, propitious, ubiquitous,
Never desultory;
He makes his way on a mission to who-knows-where,
But somehow we know that he will make it there.
What is his story? We do not know.
He's that certain somebody we've seen everywhere.
His long locks flap under his cap,
As he dons the jacket of his favorite team;
Listening to his earbuds, he is happily secluded,
Blissfully enisled.
The fixture keeps moving, with arms swinging forward,
Until his figure slowly fades on the horizon.

KIND LIGHT

His mind was fertile with vast and puerile projects,
In the main bold and incongruous with the mainstream;
There was nary a cliché regarding his mien,
Ever defying type, ever defying nomenclature.

He was agronomist, forester, poet, historian, spellbinding orator;
He departed the university, much as did the Scholar Gypsy.
Here manifested a breathing contradiction, a perplexing admixture,
An elusive vineyard of so many disparate vintages.
His bearing was unconditional, magnetic, confident,
Spiritual, yet tenuous, masking weaknesses he hid so well,
As a woodsman conceals the deep scars from his saw.
He was both loyal friend and one who sadly disappointed;
Would that I were able to reconcile such conflicting poles,
Constrained to navigate the turbulent rapids of our friendship,
As though paddling a stone canoe,
Aspiring to reach the peaceful waters of *rapprochement*.
Not having seen him for years—how shall I say?—
Our paths had followed separate ends—
I learned that he had suddenly passed;
Out, brief candle.
I then beheld in sadness his smiling photograph,
Redolent of his better angels;
In the end, I found forgiveness,
Rendering resentment into the discard,
And I chose to remember the Kind Light projected from his eyes.

A MAN MOST HUMBLE

He was always a man most humble,
Whom you could count on in difficult times,
Until the earth might crumble.

As faithfully as the church bell chimes,
He quietly shouldered every chore;
He never avoided the steepest of climbs.

Though weary, he always gave more,
Exhibiting character rare;
His fealty, always he swore.

He always had time to spare,
No matter the burdens he bore—
He took the time to care.

APOGEE

I rise in praise of humble work and charity,
For honey is extracted from the flowers
Whence the fruit comes also.
All hail an elegant champion of cumbrous deeds
Which redound to his honor;
Yet he has no desire for the fruits of his actions.
How steep are the stairs of the charitable,
Him who has low eyes?
Rich he is, of holy thought and work,
Of capacious heart and abstemious in the face of indulgence,
Employing speech of sparse motion;
His words are always cousin to his deeds.
A wide chasm separates him
From those who mistake extravagance for munificence,
And magniloquence for eloquence,
Those caught in the effluence of pride's purge,
Passionately grasping to retain
Evanescent moments of imaginary splendor;
By their fruit, we shall know them.
One man's zenith is another man's nadir;
For the vain and discontented live in archetypal envy
Of the apogee of the humble.

ECLIPSE

The audience accepted his dictums without demur;
He spoke like some latter-day Mephistopheles[4],
Skilled purveyor of a devil's bargain,
Urbane yet contemptuous, polished yet haughty,
Assuming the aspects of an ogreish villain in a fairy tale.
He nurtured among the crowd a great appetite
Which, like any appetite, fed upon itself;
Imprinted impolitic, they forswore prudence
In favor of prayers to graven images of grifters,
Maintaining a culpable tolerance of the futile and fatuous.
They all inhabited an intricate edifice of the dour and parochial;
Few understood the extent of the eclipse.

---

[4] Mythical demon character in the Faust legend

SAINT GROBIAN'S MARCH[5]

1

"We're becoming our people", the drunkard sadly mused,
As idle as a painted ship on a painted ocean;
Well has he known many a draught of ale.
"O dronke man, disfigured is thy face!" [6]
Caught in a nostalgic sojourn of rapt intoxication,
Eschewing cautionary tales of the wise,
Dazzled by a sad descent beneath garish neon lights,
He makes a tremulous tip-toe to the tavern,
His favorite haunt, populated by a raft of rapscallions
With evaporating pocketfuls of money.

2

Erelong he speaks, as arbiter of insensate conversations,
Amidst the endless gasconade of gasbags,
People who cannot be protected from themselves.
He partakes in his considerable quaffing
With his bibulous brethren and crapulous cohorts,
While careering and careening across the floor.
A panoply of picaresque personages emerges,
An assemblage worthy of the ribaldry of Jean Genet[7],
A jumble of vagabonds and hapless gypsies
Who bide their time cadging cigarettes
And telling each other's fortunes,
All smiling on their tragicomic undertakings.
Wizened faces are seated at the altar,
Where high priests dispense welcome anaesthetics
Through sacred chalices to insouciant communicants.

3

Here the cultivations of worthy pursuits
Are towers toppled by inert sloth and numbing lassitude,

---

[5] Fictional patron saint of the vulgar and coarse
[6] Chaucer, *The Canterbury Tales*
[7] French novelist; in his early life, he was a vagabond and petty criminal

Enraptured by the false glory of stumbling sensibilities,
Keenly preoccupied with jocose jabberings.
Lifeblood of the publicans, they inhabit boweries of the benighted,
Drowning grief in goblets of woebegone welters;
Lighthearted raillery sometimes descends into mockery
And the issuance of guttural imprecations.
They extol the execrable, celebrating the pathos,
Sworn in drunkenness, where dignity lies sepulchered,
Captivated by the shameful amusement of sanctified fools.
Their vision is hopelessly hazened by that most singular astigmatism,
That misshapen arc through which alcoholic eyes perceive the world.
They are long tarnished by the foul weather of experience,
Lost in a haze of misplaced reveries,
Finding sad sanctuary in what the misbegotten call delight.

TO DREAM WITH THE ANGELS

"Tonight, I lay down to dream with the angels",
So he concludes with benignant grace
The call he has made a thousand times over;
He sends kind *abrazos*[8] with a smile on his face.

He speaks with his wife and children each night—
They live in a distant Mexican village;
He works the farmlands of the faraway north;
To support them, he toils in the tillage.

In joy, he exclaims, *"Mi vida es dando",* [9]
In the land of *los norteamericanos*;
Su amor es un cenote sin fondo;
Por corazón, él obra los manos. [10]

An incomparable tale of devotion,
His life truly tells;
To sacrifice all for the ones we love—
That is to dream with the angels.

---

[8] hugs
[9] "My life is giving."
[10] His love is a bottomless well; For his heart, he works his hands.

VII. Of Human Affairs

MOTHER

1

First memory was feeling warm water from the sink as a child,
As your nurturing hands gently washed my hair;
You were thrilled when I picked for you
Bright yellow dandelion bouquets,
Placing them in vases of water.
You bandaged my scrapes, you read me stories;
You comforted me, you dried my tears,
You held my hand in sickness;
You were proud to be my protector.

2

So many years later, in your waning twilight,
I was proud to be your protector;
I wheeled you in your chair outside,
To be thrilled by the sight of bright yellow sunflowers;
Once again, I brought you bouquets,
Placing them in vases of water.
When your eyes failed, I read you stories;
I comforted you, I dried your tears,
I held your hand in sickness,
At a time when the sands were running out,
Ere your fair light had fled,
Until you took your final breath.
Last memory was kissing your kind forehead goodbye,
Praying to Our Lord Jesus, as you had taught me,
As He welcomed you into His loving World of Light.

3

What I would now give for the simple touch of your absent hand,
Or to hear the soothing sound of your vanished voice,
Now muted on earth;
Yet the tender grace of those days will never depart from me.
New seas pour into my eyes,
That I might wash the world with earnest weeping,
As I sting from all the arrows of sorrow,

Beset by dolors and lamentations of loss,
As a listing wintry willow shivering in the sun.
Would that I were steadfast in my grief,
Yearning past elegy, thirsting beyond threnody,
Wherefore I would repay the bounty you have given me.
But it is as the sky: it can never be approached.

FEIGNED JOY

When fed with the bread of affliction,
It is a strange melody to assimilate joy in rocking an empty rocking chair,
To proclaim the sad irony with tearful eyes and a smiling mouth,
Constrained to dissimulate grief and counterfeit cheer in the wake of heartbreak,
Forced to show a feigned joy.
It is an undue sadness to mask misfortunes
Which have hardened into weatherbeaten stones;
To be enjoined to endure the untold agony of choking down muted sorrow
In the face of spewed platitudes and empty apothegms;
To be obliged to blench in pain,
While donning a tenuous mask of affected well-being;
To be coerced to search for bearings in times of solitary solicitude,
As a ship without harbor, with moorings weakened and old certainties lost,
Seeking refuge in the midst of shifting tides.
Schemes go astray in the search for promised joy;
For smiles cannot be wrung from overwrought souls.

A FALSE APOLOGY

Of what value is it to extract false contrition with a crowbar?
Feigned sincerity masquerades under many guises;
With impostures too clever by half,
Some transgressors are characterized by urbane speech,
While smoking a factitious peace pipe;
They shower liberally with polite, meaningless words,
And with generous portions of laments counterfeited.
Trailing banderoles and pennons of false penance,
They are wont to parrot shopworn aphorisms and parenthetical platitudes,

Trundling forth a steady stream of worthless bromides and foolish fire,
Spewing an endless procession of sorry sonnets.
They try to filch forgiveness begotten by falsity,
Dissimulating deception under thin-lipped smiles.
Part-time astrologers dispense empty annunciations,
Vague and abstruse pronouncements of affected expiation,
As a peccant soul who stands by a river,
Pretending to empty his pockets of his sins on the Day of Atonement,
Aiming to extinguish fault through feigned contrition;
For a false apology is far worse than no apology at all.

ABIDED

They sought simple kinship at a distant place,
In hopes to be greeted by warm embrace;
Through gossamer windows, they peered inside,
From icy reception, they could not hide;
Such sadness of a stranger, sensibilities numbed:
To be abided, but not welcomed.

NO HONOR SO AUGUST

It is great folly to imagine we may control those who slander us in cold cruelty,
As though we may presume to rule the wanton winds,
Or to superintend the mutable tides of the sea.
In the end, we have but our character to possess,
That essence we hold inviolable in the face of foul spite and assault;
Violent rainstorms pelt the sea, yet the sea remains salt.
For there is no honor so august
As to be detested by the detestable.

CRACKED PRISM

I once committed the folly of following shadowy characters
Into the cupboards of their minds;
Those who accuse you of theft,
When you simply try to borrow back your own rake;
Those who are always sure to offer you an umbrella on a sunny day;

Superciliates who preach the laws of prudence
To desperate souls who push shopping carts full of empty cans;
The moralistic who extol the virtues of family,
While quarreling amongst themselves, as only blood relations can;
Those for whom slight misfortunes become grievous slights;
Those who engage in profligate spending at the expense of others;
Those who adopt postures of piety while speaking with bad intent,
Carefully crafting legalistic answers to plain moral questions;
Those who remain mute in knowing silence,
Failing to disabuse others of promulgated falsehoods,
As shameful as the invention of any lie;
Those who are spellbound by a half-baked alchemy,
Who regard the world through a cracked prism.

COMBUSTION

Even the most innocent feet tread upon an anthill by accident;
Unwitting souls are sadly availed amenities
Woven through the looms of affliction.
They are graced by the tainted raiment of fine garments spun by children;
They savor sumptuous repast from remote harvests of oppression;
For even the most benevolent and most kind
Have unknowingly partaken of the comfort of a defiled furnace,
Relishing the warmth cast by the sad combustion of dreams.

KALIMBAS

Lost denizens of moribund wonderlands, they are;
Mesmerized by their miniature hand-held screens
Are the dubious masters of the electronic thumb piano,
Relentlessly clinging to their kalimbas of no consequence.
The lost art of human interaction
Is suffused with the suffocation of hurries and lost attention spans,
With febrile focus shifting suddenly, as a football quarterback changes signals;
Like darting fishes reacting to the luminous flashes of lures,
Their fleeting thoughts are long-forgotten since the eternity of last minute;
The antidote to their acedia is their hand-held encyclopedia.

All are riveted by the appurtenances of apathy,
And by the mighty cybernetic mart;
Constrained by the tentacles of torpor and the lassos of lassitude,
They walk hypnotically, with heads firmly down,
Transfixed, opiated, oblivious, obtruding, and obtuse,
Clumsily stumbling into onwalkers
Who regard all this with puzzlement and dispraise.
It is tragically-truncated thought, devolving into thoughtless thought.

CYBERPOLEMICS

1

Devouring their brand of laudanum like moldy bread,
A petulant horde bakes its schemes in the ovens of tumult,
As they stumble through malodorous corridors,
Beset with feverish faces, muttering maledictions,
Embracing the cheap chattel of slanderous tongues.
They operate in an invisible milieu which is the obverse of decency,
Inhabiting *arrondissements* of arrogant anonymity,
Places laced with the laconic histrionics of the daft and fatuous.
They are unsuited to rational thought in the palpably worst arena,
Preaching in a manner pretentious and sententious,
Solacing themselves with graspings in asperity, so stark in severity.
Abuses expand, as abuses will do,
Subject to the relentless importunity of fools and reprobates,
Condemned to wearing cybernetic sandwich boards
Of likes and dislikes in a sad public circus.

2

The apply their mawkish keystrokes with sharpened barbs,
Preponderated by sterile audiences of willing sycophants;
With virulent vicissitudes and veriform vexations,
They are but another sad countenance of conniving calumny,
Hurling harmful projectiles of invectives and dispraise.
They abuse sacred Scripture as a brandished sword,
Defiling the Decalogue, wounding with the thorns of the Rose meant to heal.
They are purveyors of a toxic tincture, a curious curare,

While remaining immune to their own poison, like Rasputin;
They calculate contempt until their souls are fully amortized.
Cowardly-cloaked mocking supplants substance and virtue,
In deference to attacks with epistolary pistols;
They are hiding something dark and inscrutable,
Something foul concealed inside churlish skulls,
Something steeped in a bitter tea of anaesthetized sensibilities.

3

Wielding words as though halberds of medieval warriors,
They reside in the sad province of those who seek concurrence
With banal and hollow blandishments,
Counterpoised by reason, as dark against light;
They marginalize rectitude as a toothless dog
Nibbling at the crusts of warped conversations,
Where gibberish becomes reason, and reason gibberish.
They are mavens of the craven and connoisseurs of the sewer;
All of this is subject to the sordid schemes of lesser angels,
Fallen so low as to become nameless.

A GIFT OF LOVE

Moon on the horizon, rising parallax red;
It knows me better than I know my own dread.
As I empty this drawer-full of pain,
Sad and troubled fancies that I cannot explain.

My heart knows no boundaries, my heart knows no fence;
It drips Pain's icicles, and it knows no pretense.
Pursuing her love, there was no in-between—
The darkest terror, or a beautiful dream.

These wildfire emotions, they know no reproof;
They're just layers of atmosphere, obscuring knowledge, blurring truth.
I ask myself, what can all of this bring?
Icy winds are still howling, when I thought it was spring.

I follow this dream-crash on the slippery ledge,
From the Valley of the Fallen to the brink of the edge.
That razored wire's what my heart fears the most;
Sometimes my heart almost gave up the ghost.

Love produces such magnificent fools;
They understand love never follows the rules.
The darkest feeling my soul ever touched,
Is to mean so very little to one who means so very much.

Caught in a dark prison of dangerous dreams;
Lost in strange places, in a million dark streets;
I lost my way in this journey somehow,
Till I crashed on Love's highway, I drive an Illusion now.

Black echoes of loneliness in a sea of my tears;
How I miss her sweet vision—her smiling face, so clear!
I gave more than I had, I never gave enough;
I gave her more than everything;
It was a Gift of Love.

LIFTED UP

1

Once I dwelled in a house that counted me as a stranger.
My days were consumed with smoke, contemned and condemned,
Borne on contumelious connubial firestorms and hymeneal hieroglyphics,
Urgently seeking deliverance from a surging sea of lurking absurdities.
After months of futility and wearisome nights,
While my sleep fled away through hours passing slowly as tortoises,
I was plagued by the recrudescence of stubborn nightmares,
Horrible hauntings which caused me to tremble of slumber;
It was more so the fever, less so the fight, that was the weight I bore.
In the wake of somnolent sorrow dances,
As I struggled to regain purchase on my thoughts,
I inhabited a land so dark as darkness itself,
Preponderated by turbid wraiths of cruelty,
Comprehending sadly what lie hidden behind smiling masks.

And so I left that house and shook the dust from my sandals,
Fleeing in extirpation of the madness,
As if to seek the rock of escape of wild goats,
Departing in a hapless, haggard Hejira, now rendered enisled.
Get thee behind me.

2

With a suppliant heart and complaisant bearing,
I searched for the Halls of Justice,
But instead I was relegated to the Corridors of Inveigle
And the Chambers of Legerdemain;
There mercy and reason were nowhere to be found,
Where the torches of Equity long had been doused
By the foul waters of obliquity.
August marble statuary and fine mahogany benches
Conferred an outward aspect of fair play,
But perverse proceedings proved to be the obverse
Of such dignified trappings.
Through forces inimical, churlish voices fulminated against me,
Marked by mendacity and empty knowledge,
Voices punctuated by iniquitous timbre and twisted intentions.
All of this, foul personages forged in a furnace of bad faith unexampled,
Setting the off-key pitch, so that the awful coda could be composed.
My plaintive entreaties for reason went unmet;
Fleeting figures were adorned in flowing sacerdotal robes,
Rendering specious and sadistic judgments,
Grim reminders that false justice wears many cloaks.
And so I was betrayed by the tongues of the crafty,
And my case was weighed by a carnival of crooked scales.

3

Thus they devised my exiguous subsistence,
Ruling that although I had taken nothing,
Still I must restore what I did not take through distraint,
Wherefore I could not say.
As I abided the intolerable tides of unjust retrenchments,
I was consigned to a rudderless ship with a purloined helm,
Navigating concussed with a broken compass of lost verities,
Set adrift in a sea of grotesque countenances.

Soon I was surrounded by a swarm of wild bees,
Stinging me wildly as I trodded forth soberly,
As though Ezekiel wandering through the valley of the dry bones.
I was imprisoned by fruitless, circular searches,
Till I turned away from looking at worthless things;
Then I beheld the lessons which suffering illumines
As nothing else can.

4

And as I was tested in the furnace of affliction,
Then betimes I was rescued by the heights of Heaven,
Shepherding me from dark canyons to sanguine pastures;
And the cruel voices were rendered mute,
Like straw before the wind, counterpoised by angels.
I was surrounded by songs of deliverance,
As an oracle in my heart thus put all my tears in God's bottle.
I was comforted by sacred Words written long ago,
That the wicked are snared in the work of their own hands;
Then I learned of things too wonderful for me to understand,
Things which I did not know.
And so I was Lifted Up by the Lord.
Selah.

ONCE-BROKEN HEARTS

Once the day was so dark that day was but darkness made visible;
Streams of past injuries now flow through the pierced chainmail,
From misspent years of vying for the unattainable,
As lingering vestiges of snowfields in the spring.
Fleeting ancient moments persist, as biting incisors,
As strands of filaments floating through the ether,
Vexations akin to turns of thread the spiders throw across our path;
Worthless manacles strive to be shed,
In quest of aspirations otherwise inconsequent.
To walk the path of those with dashed dreams:
Do not judge harshly the capitulations of once-broken hearts.

SHIELD

As the harsh hand of random hazardry exercised its capricious will,
The cruel sting of the cast dice befell his desperate circumstance;
His shocked countenance was rendered pendulous.
Ill-timed tragedy summoned a rush to derogate dreams,
As though pulling out weeds, as though stripping away detritus,
Settling into a moment of sheer weakness,
Buttressed by that impervious shield,
That which betrays the vision of clear eyes;
Such is the price of soothing illusion,
As if ingested white wisps of numbing opium.
But the clearest of clear voices exhorted me:
Do not take away his shield.

READING GÖETHE

She writes of deep romance,
In travel, her words, they dance,
Speaking their unspoken trance
Of her love for me.
But these same things, I do not feel,
Her heart, I dare not steal;
I cannot feign what is not real,
It is what it will be.

She holds me in a lofty place,
Magic written on her face,
She gives her heart in heavy haste;
This, I did not ask.
No sooner than her words extol,
Her plaudits turn to vitriol,
As quickly as hot turns to cold;
I cannot wear the mask.

I know too well the other side,
As I hear the storm outside,
The lightning, I will not deride;

It alarms me so.
I sit inside, reading Göethe,
About *The Sufferings of Young Werther*;
How much it hurts to be the hurter,
How much I've come to know.

For there is nothing I can do,
But to be hard and true;
To own her heart, I cannot do;
I must be harsh and kind.

PAIRINGS

Some marry for the cause of linked nobility,
As concords for alliances of state.
Some race against the waning of fertility;
They cast their choices to the winds of Fate.

For some, no doubt, their hormones make their choices;
They do their thinking well below the waist.
While others simply mute their inner voices;
They're most content with friendship in their haste.

Some wed for riches, seeking only wealth;
Portfolios exalt from high above.
And sometimes, if by chance or if by stealth,
Some marry for the cause of burning love.

PERSUASION

Capitulating at first summons to persuasive charms,
Inexplicable, and even in hindsight remaining so;
Loving without quite knowing why,
Ensnared by a congenial mysticism,
With whispers of walking in perilous ways.

SECRETS

With charms of love, the sharpest sight does blur
The sad occlusions which perforce arise;
A willing heart won't waver or demur;
So credulous are love-afflicted eyes.

Through false love, one cannot see,
When foolish fancy renders blind;
But when one sees while walking free,
One sees all secrets of the mind.

FRIENDSHIP

For true friendship,
Commitment is neither strained nor parsimonious;
There is no order too tall, nor patience too short—
No caveats, no qualifications, no exceptions, no fine print.
There is no hospitality withheld, nor is any grudge held;
There is no faith too fatiguing,
No kindness too crushing,
No sacrifice too severe,
No succor too stringent,
No tenderness too tenuous,
No ardor too arduous.
True friendship transcends the tribal
And erases resentment;
It cherishes differences with acceptance
And renders envy into the discard;
Beseeching of a favor is not necessary;
There is no devotion too imprudent,
No love too immoderate,
For true friendship.

FORGOTTEN BY FEET

I traveled to a place forgotten by feet,
Greeted by the outstretched arms of old friends;
My spirit was weakened, welded by heat,
Forged in the crucible of lost amends.

I went to the spring, I leaned on the pump,
I fetched jugs of water for evening repast;
I took axe in hand, split wood on the stump;
Through such simple chores, new peace came at last.

We sat down inside at dimming of day,
Warmed at hearthside, glowing amber and red;
We spoke of the years which had vanished away;
After fine banquet, I retired to bed.

How to describe that kindness so bright,
Of that glowing white candle's soft diffused light?

WHOM IT DAZZLES

1

They are reared on golden hobby horses,
Conveyed by palanquins of privilege, holding sway over seigneurial realms;
As the Great Mogul, they receive their weight in gold balances.
Comfortably ensconced in remote palatial estates out on Post Card Road,
With cultivated proclivities, they stroll through manicured greenswards
And saunter through arbored garden walkways,
Passing through august archways marked by elegant ogival curves,
Leading them into capacious halls framed by gilded walls and marble pilasters.
Prodigals dine on fine silver plates in princely fashion,
Adorned in frippery, dressed in fine silk of scarlet,
Trimmed with sashes of rich sable and white ermine,
Embellished by coruscating jewels;
Butter would not melt in their mouths.

97

2

Breathing mannequins in *manteaux* are bedecked
With the showy habiliments of cosmopolites,
Banqueting together with great *hauteur* and satiety,
Amidst the incessant popping of champagne corks,
Replete with grandiloquent exchanges of self-congratulatory toasts.
Decorous legatees of leisure dance to the music of the spheres of influence,
Feted with an endless parade of staid cotillions,
Amid frenzied huzzahs, affording themselves every *plaisance*.
They are waxed in wealth, waned in honor,
Lost in fantastic and useless schemes,
Quenching their thirsts from the fountains of emoluments.

3

Masters of pretension, they savor the snifters of prerogative,
As old marble heads bear honorific titles and multiple middle initials;
They struggle for trivial distinctions between social castes,
Separated only by adventitious demarcations.
They are exponents of extravagance, proponents of opulence;
Their ostentatious refinements border on ridiculous,
As they conduct urbane battles of aureate rhetoric,
Waged with perfunctory smiles and outward courtesies,
Measuring out their days in libation cups of fine crystal.
Coveting Croesus[11], they are cornered by the false meditations of frigid minds,
Remaining immune to the corrections of experience.

4

They are destined in the end for catafalques of carved dark mahogany
And colonnaded mausoleums of fine white marble.
But when the gold rusts, what shall they do?
How then shall the world be served?
Of what avail shall be earthly mammon?
How shall worldly grandeur be measured by Heaven's treasuries?
Temporal fortunes are tenuously soldered
To the odd camouflage of ephemeral secularities;

---

[11] Wealthy king of ancient Greece, whose pride destroyed his own kingdom

Bright beacons illuminate the concealment,
Then a new style becomes another mask;
For beauty deceives its owner, more than whom it dazzles.

MARIONETTE

On the opposite side of a chasm from a pearl-maiden, I once stood,
In pilgrimage, as though to Compostela; [12]
In quest of leaping miracles, risking everything in hazardry,
I ventured to swim across the Hellespont. [13]
With gladsome mind, in diffidence, bleakly and obliquely,
I endeavored to shield myself from blazing meteor showers
Of her sharp unrequittance,
But I could not hide from that searing light.
I wheedled for the guerdon of her elusive affections,
Under the alders with tremulous shuddering,
Relinquishing the reliquaries of caution and prudence,
Abiding countless stings while seeking honeyed apiaries,
Importuning deaf dcities to no avail.
All of this garnered dismissal and dispraise (so it seemed),
All unfolding in ghastly perfection;
Would that I were able to extinguish my foolishness with reason,
But to be dispatched to wander otherwhere through a barren dream,
Carrying a lit candle in supplication,
Where the conjuror played as it all redounded upon me;
I was barely able to stand on my feet.
Erelong it had me dancing as a sad marionette,
Painted face frowning as the lightning flashed therewith,
Strings entangled, floundering and foundering.
In the end, discountenanced while bound in surety,
Yet with dignity somehow rescued,
I suffered only lingering doubt as to the next time—
Loosen the cross-brace, disentangle the strings,
Apply the unguents, maintain a feeble echo in the heart;
Risk again the wonderful mistake of cherishing immoderate dreams.

---

[12] Spanish city of Santiago de Compostela, burial site of Biblical apostle St. James
[13] In Classical Antiquity, name of the Dardanelles Strait, in present-day Turkey

VIII.   Of History, Traditions, and Folklore

THERE HISTORY STANDS

1

We see through a glass darkly;
Mysterious is the evidence of history.
We see journals of those busy making and unmaking emperors,
Memoirs of corteges for kings, reminders of fleeting earthly stations;
We read tales of mausoleums of princes, short-sighted monuments to the ephemeral;
Apices of achievement appear, attained and forgotten,
Once noted, then quietly dissipated, as a vanishing voice's echo in a canyon,
Borne of sacred rites of a remote past, now obsequies for days long evaporated.

2

There history stands, bound up in gilt volumes,
Chronicling the events of the ages,
Placing flowers in the cemeteries of empires;
The ancients recounted things which were ancient in their own day.
Looking backward for lessons through a hazy lens,
Indeed we see no paucity of parallels in context;
We read accounts of a time when scribes foolishly imagined
That kings and wars and statesmen alone were history;
We behold the dynastic descriptions
Of the storming of cities and the subjugation of kings.

3

But what of the questions of the great humanity?
Who shall tell of what common people did, thought, suffered, and enjoyed?
How they lived and had their being,
All the while unnoticed by those who penned the gilt volumes?
Let us explore such remote past people,
The unnamed and indiscernible masses, now long asleep in unknown graves,
Absent from chronicles once carved beneath painfully-laboring goose quills.
We endeavor to pierce the clouds of verse, to discern the real life of an epoch,
All in the quest to praise obscure men and women,
Those who begat us.

We are availed stray glimmers of ancient smiling eyes, long turned to dust,
Yet infinitely more important once than the written word that remains.
Words are lost in dreams of past perfection,
Immanent narratives awaiting a fertile seedtime,
Emendations chasing the phantasms of illusory heroic beings.
We piece through the multitudes of scattered clues of vanished emperies,
As piecing together disparate potsherds at a remote archeological dig.
Churches, houses, and bridges all tell their story,
As plainly as print for those who have eyes to read;
The Roman villa and the Druid temple, excavated after lying lost for centuries,
Bring home ancient life more clearly than any codex or textbook,
More eloquently than a hundred transcripts of those times.
To bury such worthy examples in silence is to injure posterity, to scathe civilization.

5

Some narratives were given to the vicissitudes of their time,
As though regarding the troubled sea with its changing hues,
Surveying the world through the tinted glass of their misperception;
Some enjoy a borrowed sepia-toned light in their august decrees,
But the glory of the originators remains forever.
We look back through the corridors of the ages,
Importuning those before us to avert known calamities;
But alas, we receive no answer nor echo.
We struggle to resolve the ineluctable ambiguities of retrospection,
Akin to that odd sonic distortion emitted by a garbled sound whizzing by us,
Muffled in motion to our ears through time and distance.
We take that ineffable look backward in order to guide us forward,
As if to scry through a crystal.
Will our descendants someday scoff at our blindness?
As events in a person's life, so is history:
For when we look back again, we realize that it is not the same.

FOLKWAYS

I ply the perdurable folkways,
A world awash with beauty, and heavy with delights;
The momentary glamor, I have come to see as tinsel.
In a bottomless ocean, many have sounded in vain for a spot to cast anchor;
Countless souls now inherit old places, precious vestiges of golden heydays;
They remain sadly unaware of the erasure of things past,
Things now buried in the gardens of their houses.

Do not raze monuments inviolable, nor bulldoze the patrimonial,
In deference to ephemeral worthless things;
Hold fast to sacred traditions of substance,
That numinous elegance which endures,
Even when the shade of great eras has faded away;
Regard bygone treasures with kind, commemorative eyes.

CONSECRATED

Their announcement came swift and sudden:
Our church, they plan to deconsecrate;
The church that our immigrant grandparents built—
Now we have met this sad fate.

This church holds our sacred stories,
A place of our spiritual union,
Of numberless Masses and weddings and funerals—
The place of my First Communion.

Some see just a silent edifice,
A building that's crumbling and dated;
If it cannot be saved, then close it if you must—
But you cannot deconsecrate the consecrated.

PEALING BELLS

I was once entranced by pealing bells,
The familiar voices of long ago,
Wondrous emanations from towering campaniles,
Antiphonal carillons, the timeless call of the angelus,
Rung in steady measurement of unhurried time,
The sounds of simplicity and innocence.
Whereupon I traveled, as though through the air,
Like a blackbird or thrush, in a transport of happiness,
Seeking to return to the perfection of an imaginary past,
To leave behind a troubled world,
Knocked about by petty constables,
Bobbing on the waters of temporal inconstancy,
In hopes of simple deliverance—
Somehow to return to the certainty of those bells.

BACK IN MY HOMETOWN

Last night I dreamed I saw the river,
It wound its way through my hometown;
The penny of the year I left there
Has turned from copper now to brown.
I heard the sounds of children's laughter,
Where childhood memories abound;
We played along that winding river,
Back in our day, back in my hometown.

Remember Main Street during Christmas,
Bright lights festooned across the street;
Skating at nighttime on the mill pond,
The smiling faces we would meet.
The fishing derby on the mill pond
Brought every single kid in town;
The times we stormed the old Strand Theater,
Back in our day, back in my hometown.

The time has passed away so strangely;
It moves like shadows in the cold;

Echoes and dust are now on Main Street;
Hardscrabble streets with hard-luck souls.
With a scintilla of pure kindness,
Remember all those ancient sounds;
I swear that sometimes I still hear them,
Back in our day, back in my hometown.

THE OLD SCHOOLHOUSE

Among the alders there lies an old schoolhouse,
Its weathered brick walls rest atop a small hill;
A bearer of tales so ancient and many,
Its blackboard stands silent in the classroom still.

The blackboard bears witness to the teacher's old lessons,
Inscribed once in chalk, though erased long ago;
Yet still may be seen the inscrutable traces,
Faint outlines of that which we no longer know.

We close our eyes now to see all their faces,
As only our vision of mind may allow;
Young pupils who sat here are no longer with us,
Yet still they inhabit this classroom somehow.

Today the old schoolhouse suspires yet repurposed,
Occupied now with reverence and grace,
As new feet traverse these storied worn floorboards—
Such is the magic of sanctified space.

HANDSOME LAKE

Handsome Lake was a prophet,
And he taught all across the land,
Ways of peace and understanding,
To those of every nation and every clan,
To those of every nation and clan.

In the Seneca Nation,
He was born of the Turtle Clan;
He became a great sachem;
The Western Gate was what the Nations called his land,
The Western Gate was his land.

Then he fell to the whiskey,
He sought solace in the trader's rum;
It was dissolute living
That brought him to the deathbed where he had come,
The deathbed where he had come.

Then he saw a great vision,
The Creator revealed his plan;
Then he rose from his deathbed,
And he preached in every longhouse across the land,
In every longhouse 'cross the land.

He became a great teacher,
His code he taught across the land,
Temperance, love, and compassion;
And the medicine he brought tamed a troubled land,
He tamed the trouble in his land.

Then he went to Onondaga[14],
He fulfilled what he had prophesied;
There he gave up his spirit,
And he went to his new world high above the sky,
He went to his new world in the sky.

Then they held a ceremony,
In the longhouse, they sang his song;
And then said the head preacher,
"The wind, it always dies when I sing that song,
The wind dies when I sing that song."

Handsome Lake was a prophet.

---

[14] One of the Iroquois nations

A TALE OF ACADIE

1

In the land of Acadie, in times of old,
Lies a place from where this tale must be told;
Many bright souls braved the high seas from France,
To seek the New World, so they ventured in chance.
There was a bold Frenchman named Claude Laurent,
His fur trapping trade left him no want;
Bearing hirsute visage, and of most sturdy build,
A coat of brown buckskin, his frame amply filled.
Now Acadie was under French domain,
Till Wolfe vanquished Montcalm on Abraham's plain;
The conquering British demanded a pledge
To yield to the Crown, so they pushed to the edge
The abiding Frenchmen, who now faced conscription:
Bend a knee to *Angleterre*[15], or face eviction.
Those who resisted were shipped off by boat,
To be then transported to regions remote;
But Claude was among the ones who evaded
Such a cruel fate from those who invaded;
His would-be captors gave Claude ample chase,
But Claude knew the woods better than his own face;
And so, their pursuit, he amply eluded,
Leaving them puzzled, as they thusly brooded.
Our Claude so fled their sad persecution;
In the Micmac[16] language, he had fine elocution;
He therefore escaped into forest so deep,
Where his Micmac friends gave him shelter to keep.

2

And so Claude dwelt in a Micmac village,
Where he worked with the men in hunting and tillage.
One day he espied a young Micmac squaw;
She was the loveliest creature he ever saw.
With bearing angelic and manner demure,

---

[15] England
[16] Native American tribe indigenous to the Acadian region of Canada

Her soft smile exuded a kindness so pure;
She was slender of build with straight sable hair,
Which framed her kind features, so striking and fair;
She wore a loose necklace of leather and beads;
She showed Claude affection in words and in deeds.
This maiden and Claude fell so deep in romance,
As their kind conversation would greatly enhance;
Claude spoke in Micmac, in courting his squaw,
While his maiden soon learned how to speak *Quebecois.*[17]
In that fair Micmac village, soon they were wedded,
Their love for each other so deeply embedded;
It's said that they held their sweet conjugal rite,
Reciting their vows in a manner so bright,
First in Micmac, then in *Quebecois*,
With the bride's name recorded as "*Marie Dubois*",
Or "Marie of the Woods", as it's properly said,
Marie's name invented the day they were wed.
Claude and Marie shared a fine life henceforth,
Raising their family in the land of the north;
So lived my forbears in old Acadie,
Yet still alive, somehow still here with me.

OPŁATEK[18]

Once I fell spellbound in a deep Slavic dream,
Transfixed by visions of the Infant of Prague,
Glowing in the dark, effulgent to my eyes.
In the midst of this, I visited times past,
When we celebrated the *Wigilia*[19],
To mark the Star's appearance in the sky,
Worthy of a tale by Konrad, our companionable bard,
As with Scotland's Burns and Ireland's Yeats.
We broke the *opłatek* wafer after dinner,
To wish each other health and good cheer;
I then awoke, wishing somehow to go back there,
Back to those dear times of elemental peace,
A peace well understood by all who broke the *opłatek* together.

---

[17] Dialect of French spoken in Canada
[18] Wafer used in Polish Christmas Eve tradition; pronounced "op-WAH-tek"
[19] "Vigil"; specifically, the traditional Polish Christmas Eve vigil

THE GEOGRAPHY OF NOWHERE

They would knock down Stonehenge to erect a strip mall.
Scores of cloverleafs are stamped sterile across the highways,
Homogenized wastelands of numbing false comfort.
Once-vibrant downtown streets of rich traditions have been replaced
By sprawling garish neon retail shrines,
Strangely metamorphosed into sad black asphalt patchworks
Of cloned antiseptic mercantile manifestations.
Erstwhile clusters of character are now supplanted
By insipid templates of sameness,
Constructed in pursuit of some warped will-o'-the-wisp,
Devoid of community, sadly assuaged by a curious ennui.
Memories of the corner store die quietly,
Discarded into the dim closets of history,
Dissevered as paralyzed spectral ghosts.

IX. Of World Affairs and the Commonweal

FIELDS OF THE FALLEN

Here comes now the sunrise, the daylight we greet;
Our poor feet, they walk down each bleak, barren street.
Each road that we travel, each day we begin,
We're scorched by the sun, and we're swept by the wind.

Gray fields of the fallen now cover our land;
Our homes are in ruin, our blood soaks the sand;
Our faces are weary, you know not our names;
We're different from you, but we're also the same.

We roam through our homeland, as poor as can be;
Cold, tired, and hungry, like strangers, are we;
We wade through this wasteland, we fall to our knees,
While you watch life and death on your wide-screen TVs.

The violence surrounds us, we're trapped in this fight;
The bombs keep exploding through day and through night.
We witness the horrors of each one who dies,
As we gaze at the stare of our dead children's eyes.

All through the cold mountains and hot desert sands,
We're ghosts of a war that has torn through our land;
We pray to dear God for our life yet to be;
May the fields of the fallen someday not be.

WINDS OF DESOLATION

1

During the cruelest month of the cruelest year,
I heard a people who wept with a loud voice;
It is the season for heavy rain,
And they are not able to stand outside.

Violent winds of desolation are blowing in the wilderness.
I saw a great sadness, borne of intemperance against an entire people,
Cauterized into their collective heart.

Great evils formed the edifice of their attackers,
Constructed through contempt of honor,
Inveighing against the forces of nobility,
Countervailed by the weight of somber melancholy,
Beholding the stark footprints of misfortune.
Madness and malevolence were manifested
When homes, schools, and hospitals
Became bombed-out morgues and charnel houses.
War as well as peace has its laws; arms cannot be borne against children.
Yet I saw young children and infants murdered,
With the sad detritus of their strewn shredded toys
Displayed amidst destroyed homes,
Evidence of vile crimes which were the envy of Satan;
Earth trembled from her entrails.

2

I beheld a land attacked by heartless hussars of hellish intention,
Marked by diabolical sojourns into barbaric netherworlds,
Wastelands marked by fire and smoke.
All are victims of a permanent hostility
Which treaties may plaster over, but cannot extinguish.

Then I saw an elderly woman
Who was speaking a language which I did not understand,
And yet I understood.
She was sobbing, her careworn, wizened face awash with tears;
She simply said that she wanted to go home, to sleep in her own bed again.
In that moment, I saw my own mother in her, and I began to weep bitterly.
And then my heart was moved,
As are the trees of the woods, moved with the wind;
And so I remained resolute, never to be callous to the madness.

THE HALLS OF RANCOR

Excuse my unbridled candor,
But it is required in the face of unbridled rancor.
What is to be of Man's inhumanity toward Man?
We see the implacable forces of intolerance which cannot be tolerated—
Those who despise all differences, despising even the right to be different;

Those who regard the world with covered eyes and covered ears;
Those who boast honorific titles as champions of freedom,
All the while stripping away freedom from others;
Those who adorn themselves with laurels of spiritual purity,
While extolling racial purity;
Those who clutch the Bible to their hearts,
While blinding their hearts to its sacred teachings;
Those who trundle forth their worthless wares in broken carts;
Those who reach for ancient swords,
Now rusted into the scabbards of vanished conquistadors.
A terrible reptile abides coiled in the dark corners of mankind unkind,
An abject sentinel-beast which guards the halls of rancor.

WHEN SHADOWS FALL

Once silence fell, there was a sudden hush;
A speechless grief so froze all hearts.
The autumn leaves fell early that year;
Sweet breezes were followed by chilling winds,
Subjected to the heartless whims of the demented.
The innocent were haunted by hardbitten leitmotifs,
Unleashed by catenations of madness;
Unspeakable horrors arrived from strange sources,
As alarming portents of yet new torrents approached,
Beckoning shelters heretofore shunned.

What becomes of a world where children must feign death,
In order to escape it?
What happens after the camera crews leave,
After the yellow caution tape comes down?
What of the young taken so soon,
Whose petals die before fulfilling the promise of the fruit?
And where were their guardians?
Their futile jaws sadly moved in the void,
Taking meaningless bites in the empty air,
Only then to metamorphose into stone.

We seek auguries of things yet to be revealed,
As we are besieged by the cruel incubus of hatred and fear;
What darkness finds when shadows fall.

LOS INMIGRANTES

Do not forget to entertain strangers, unwittingly entertaining angels;
Do not forget that your forbears were also strangers in a new land.

And so they departed and betook themselves to a foreign land,
Uprooted humanity thrown pell-mell
To live amongst an alien people for the rest of their lives;
Whereupon they saw the powerful oppress the weak,
And every species of wicked flourished.
All of this, they beheld at their collective distress,
As families were heartlessly rended apart,
As through dry kindling violently split by an axe,
Many never to be reunited again.
Regarded as chattel, dispatched as detritus,
They were accidental protagonists
In a strange tale of proscription and expulsion.
They sublimated their desperate dreams
To the will of twisted kings and their churlish minions;
They saw the tainted egg out of which were hatched such scurrilous schemes.
They now only wish to forge unifying filaments in a furnace of chaos,
Lost and unrecognizable in the unctuous jumble,
Facing penury and the distraint of their humanity.

TOWN SQUARE

1

I could never navigate the halls of nonsense,
Until I later learned to speak that language.
Mindful of the mindless,
I visited places propelled by rudderless verities,
Where more is meant than meets the ear,
Where Diogenes[20] searches in vain with his lantern.
I saw televised cheapjacks, architects of preconcerted tumults,
Cultivating calamities and mining mendacities,
Faint auguries of what was to follow.
They decant dark teas of temerity, boiled and steeped in confusion;

---

[20] Ancient Greek philosopher, notorious for carrying around a lantern in search of an honest man

They are masters of inveigle and invective,
Inhabiting *arrondissements* of arrogance;
They tell lies like a pastime, while confusing the armory with the sacristy;
They are given to pettifogging mountains of consequence
With anthills of insensate distractions;
They are interlocutors of daft discussions,
Occupying their days lighting tinderboxes of alarming passions,
Constructing castles of calumny with mirthless laughter.

2

Madness came to town one day, and found a welcome home.
I saw the vivisection of souls, cast in the hard molds of oblivion,
With decency discarded like glacial moraine.
I heard strident voices shriek in unctuous tongues,
As a curtain rose in an ill-conceived play;
Benedictions collided with curses,
As exalted lies were received by eager ears, all with the blindest credulity;
The voices plunged deeper into a sea of malefaction,
The depths of which are not easily sounded.
They harvested from bitter vineyards, extolling execrable vintages;
They winked their eyes to devise perverse things.
The throng could not hear distant shouts of wisdom
For the din which preempted their ears,
Elevating false idols to messianic heights.
Truculent and truckling,
They pillaged sacred shrines in the false posture of worshipers,
Attacking with medieval halberds and mailed fists;
Their makeshift gallows were warped cenotaphs
To the sacred sacrifices of the countless many.
Such a disgrace was unexampled.
In the morrow, while many mourned the malice,
Others shielded their eyes with resolved indifference,
Retreating to the comfort of primitive fables;
They remained faithless, abjuring reason,
Paying heed to those who supplant creed with screed,
Trading courts of wise counsel for synods of sycophants,
Where somewhere is nowhere, and nowhere is somewhere.
As sad voices of reason echoed out of empty cisterns,
All had changed utterly.
And so it goes.

Ought not calm voices be raised amid the tumult?
Am I your enemy simply because we disagree?
Liberty, the word rings so sweet; we must clasp it before it fades.
I proclaim my supplication to Heaven, to calm intemperate seas,
To release the jammed wheels of history,
That truth might find purchase and spring again.
The fallen leaves have landed on the lakes of languor;
The avenues of perdition are lined with listing laurels.
Desperate countenances are illumined by the faint glow of fading dreamlights;
Some render past ideals into sterile stone statuary,
Consigned to pale alabaster, silent and lifeless;
Disconsolate souls still search for the fruits of past promises,
Sandblasting the soot off the Minuteman in the Town Square.

I WONDER

I wonder why humanity's so low;
I wonder, what I'm seeing, is it so?
I wonder why the winds of evil blow;
They're blowing over you.

I wonder of the horrors of the souls;
I wonder where the screams of silence go;
I wonder why the winds of evil blow;
They're blowing over you.

I wonder why the death-tears ever flow;
I wonder what we all will come to know;
I wonder why the winds of evil blow;
They're blowing over you.

Written on September 11, 2001

X.   Humorous Musings

A LONG LIFE

A lawyer once quietly passed away;
On planet Earth, she could no longer stay.
Soon she arrived at Heaven's gate,
Awaiting there shortly to learn of her fate.

Saint Peter perused his voluminous book—
For the lawyer's name, so he did look;
He then did a double-take, acting nonplussed—
Very seldom it happened, that he had so fussed.

He quickly assembled a conclave of saints,
Who rendered applause with a lack of restraints;
In Heaven, this sort of assemblage is rare;
It's only summoned for the fairest of the fair.

The attorney was stunned as a humble visitor;
For Pete's sake, she was a simple solicitor.
The stunning display of applause so embarrassed her,
Not being a saint—she was only a barrister.

Saint Peter advised where he placed his reliance:
"We've tallied the hours you've billed all your clients;
It's all quite remarkable, may it be told—
You've lived to be over two hundred years old!"

TO BE THERE (OR NOT TO BE THERE)

The audience sat and awaited the start of the play;
The director then took center stage with something to say.
His announcement was sudden, if even a bit controversial:
"Our Hamlet ran off to New York to do a commercial."

THE DOCTOR'S VISIT

A woman went to the doctor one day,
To see what the doctor would have to say;
Her painful malady, so it did roil—
On her buttocks, she had a terrible boil.

She thusly entered the medical building;
Each doctor's name was listed in gilding.
She promptly entered the very first door,
Which displayed the name of "Doctor Moore".

Upon her entrance, it was a great boon,
To encounter a doctor so very soon;
She thus bared her buttocks for the doctor's inspection,
To which he repaired with the keenest detection.

He told her, "This warrants a second opinion;
I think you should show this to Doctor Finnan."
And so he directed her several doors down;
To see the next doctor, she went with a frown.

The second doctor, he took a close look;
He examined the boil, as his head, so he shook;
He judged, "This case needs another referral.
Go straight down the hall to see Doctor Farrell."

With this directive, the patient complied,
Although her chagrin, she could now barely hide;
And so this third doctor, he took a long peek,
Only to tell her, "Return here next week."

Upon her exit from said establishment,
She chanced to encounter the superintendent;
She related to him her most odd experience,
To which he replied with discomfort and deference:

"The building is under complete restoration;
Everything's closed due to this renovation."
The unfortunate news, he did so confide:
"Only the painters are working inside."

MY FAVORITE WOOD

Whenever I golf, one thing that is good,
I've always treasured my favorite wood;
It's truly one of my favorite things—
Many less strokes on my scorecard, it brings.

My driver can really hit the ball far,
Though, last time I used it, I demolished a car;
The loft from my three-wood is really tops,
But the ball, right into the water, it plops.

My favorite wood saves me many a stroke;
Just look at my scorecard, it isn't a joke.
My favorite wood is— don't think me a louse—
That little pencil they give out at the clubhouse.

DAY JOB

Spinoza made his living grinding lenses;
His writings earned a dearth of recompenses.
Chaucer worked in service to the Crown;
His Tales had not yet garnered his renown.
Fielding was a barrister in court;
His authorship could not provide support.
Caillebotte was a wealthy engineer;
His paintings couldn't pay his bills so dear.
Whitman was reporter for a paper;
A poet's wages vanish in the vapor.
Hawthorne's job was at the Custom House;
He worked there to maintain a happy spouse.
Kafka worked insurance, with a shrug;
He prayed that he'd awaken as a bug.

We all have to eat.

RIDICULOUS PROBLEMS

Some twist into knots, while seeking resolutions,
Partaking in elaborate ablutions;
No mystery, why we face such convolutions—
Ridiculous problems require ridiculous solutions.

ANAESTHETIC

I asked the apothecary to dispense a curative
For painful interactions with the rude and rebarbative;
He told me, in regards to such behavior pathetic,
Absence is the only proven anaesthetic.

DENIZEN

The swift departure of a fleeting concept
Becomes the very fabric of the precept.
Lost thoughts escape, they flee beyond our ken:
Forgetfulness, the denizen of Zen.

NAMASTE

Legions of visitors arrive in their state of illeisure,
Rude to delicious quiet and solitude,
Honking their horns with grimaced, fractured faces,
All in a hurry to relax, slavish to clocks,
And hell-bent on enlightenment.
Some fiends spoil even paradise;
Gotta get there quick,
Or they might miss out on nirvana—
Namaste, get the hell outta the way!

CHARADES

The Queen of Sheba shielded shy Charlemagne
From a shell game shilled by a shifty shaman
With a big schnoz, the schmegegge of schlemiels.
Charlatans and shams shunned the shibboleths,
As chivalrous shepherds schlepped their shabby schmutz,
Shedding their chevron neckties and Shetland shawls,
Then shivering as sherpas served them fine shirahs.
Shouting schlimazels emptied their shelves in closed shops,
While shameless showboats shuffled off with their schatzis
To the surefire shindig,
Sipping champagne on a shoestring budget.
Shoguns left their shacks to walk their schnauzers,
As they gave short shrift to the shoddy,
While emerging from the shadows.
Shalom.

PEDANT'S INDULGENCE

Osiris was hangin' out with the fellahs,
While Jeremiah delivered a jeremiad;
He speculated before he peculated.
The varlet wore scarlet, and the jerk wore a jerkin;
The tocsins warned of toxins, as the jilter drank a philter.
The goon was jejune when Philip got a fillip;
He wrote an epithelium with delirium, as the subaltern held a lantern.
The hypocrite drank hippocras, as the *alguazil* showed his zeal,
While the horse's caparison was beyond comparison.
The polymath was a polyglot, the Tory was hortatory,
The harquebusier was busier, and the dentist was an irredentist.
The novice poets were still inchoate;
After they were sated, they tergiversated.
They thought their peroration brought adulation;
Contrariwise, they were all despised.
This concludes this daft bit of poesy—
That is to say, it's a *fait accompli.*

BABY BOOMER'S INDULGENCE

Sherman, set the Wayback Machine
Back to Route 66, Car 54, and Stalag 13,
And Flip Wilson as Geraldine.

Put the rabbit ears antenna on top of the TV,
I'm gonna tell you how it's gonna be,
See Zorro, who makes the sign of the Z.

Wear your hair in a bun, like the Flying Nun,
She's come undun, and we'll have fun, fun, fun,
Phasers on stun, we've only just begun.

Pick you up at eight, and don't be late,
Or you'll get the Fickle Finger of Fate,
From Grandpa Amos, Luke, and Kate.

What's up, doc? Yabba-dabba-doo!
Tell Howdy Doody and Captain Kangaroo
I took my troubles down to Madame Rue.

Mantle & Maris, Drysdale & Koufax,
Agent 99 & Max, and Peter Max—
The facts, ma'am, just the facts.

Sheriff Taylor and Uncle Tonoose,
Mr. Green Jeans and Mr. Moose,
In the midnight hour, I can't turn you loose.

Come and listen to a story 'bout a man named Jed—
You better head back to Tennessee Jed—
There's a signpost ahead, I am Mister Ed.

Creepy Crawlers and Jonny Quest,
Chatty Cathy and Father Knows Best,
The Shady Rest and the Wild, Wild West.

Eenie Meanie, Chili Beanie,
Bewitched, I dream of Jeannie,
Wearing an itsy-bitsy, teenie-weenie, yellow polka dot bikini.

The Good Humor Man, American Bandstand,
Lost in Fantasyland with…
Ginger or Mary Ann?

Tie-dyed shirts at the Woodstock Fair,
Love beads and a bean bag chair,
Gimme a head with hair, long, beautiful hair.

I forgot, to tell the truth… what's my line?
Number nine… number nine…
Quit listening in on the party line!

Groovy, out of sight, far out,
Twist and shout, let it all hang out.

Hula Hoops, Silly Putty, Slinky,
And chemistry sets so stinky.

Don't you know that the bird's the word?
Always shaken, never stirred.

He loves TV, that Arnold Ziffel the Pig—
He digs watching Hullabaloo and Shindig.

Cassius Clay, Sugar Ray, and Murray the K,
What I'd say, that'll be the day.

Ivan Putski and Chief Jay Strongbow,
Do the limbo, how low can you go?

Said Andy Warhol to Dorothy Hamill,
I'd walk a mile for a Camel.

Wilt the Stilt, Russ, Sam & K.C.,
McHale and the crew of PT 73.

Paladin, Paladin, where do you roam?
Kookie, Kookie, lend me your comb, oh Lucy, I'm home.

Carrie Ann, Barbara Ann, Lucille, and Claudette—
Look at that Tod Stiles, driving that Corvette!

Sky pilot, how high can you fly?
Eight miles high, goin' up to the spirit in the sky.

One giant leap for Neil Armstrong—
Hey Mr. Spaceman, won't you please take me along?

Mercury, Gemini, Apollo,
And where he goes, I'll follow.

John, Paul, George, and Ringo,
Surfin' USA, Beach Blanket Bingo.

Papa's got a brand new bag,
But mama told me not to come—rag, mama, rag.

Look what they've done to my song, ma—
I don't need no wah-wah.

Like a bird on a wire, light my fire,
McGuinn & McGuire still a-gettin' higher.

Move over, Rover, let Jimi take over,
Checkmate King 2, this is White Rook, over.

What, me worry? said the joker to the thief—
Can you surry? Sorry about that, Chief.

You don't need a weatherman to know…
I've been warped by the rain, driven by the snow…

I wish I was homeward bound,
But I'm feeling like Charlie Brown,
Looking for a shortcut he never found.

Somewhere beyond the sea,
There will be an answer, let it be.

Is that all there is? Is that all…
Better consult the eight ball:
Reply hazy, try again.
This is the end, beautiful friend.

Seems as though I only briefly dozed…
Well, King, this case is closed.

There is nothing wrong with your television set—
Good night, David, good night Chet.
Napoleon Solo, open Channel D:
Now it's time to say goodbye to all our company.

XI.   Of Dreams, Magic, and Mysticism

THE ATOMS OF DREAMS

1

In the mystical destinations of dreams,
When the eaves of half-dropped eyelids succumb to the sacred balm of slumber,
Slowly retreating behind the opaque curtain,
We access that vast, submerged continent, illumined by a few pinpoints of light.
We inhabit hazy landscapes of alien associations,
Traveling that untraveled world of random connections and remote personages,
Dealt swiftly by the mysterious hand of chance.
Unlikely characters clamber forth in their humors as curious thespians;
Blurred phantasms ostensibly ossify into concrete beings,
Appearing in cloudy, hibernating histrionics,
All staged in a strange milieu of our own making.
Everything unfolds in uncanny plots and adventitious adventures,
A confused jumble of dizzying atmospherics
And gathered sheafs, inane and incondite,
As though the haphazard fancies of tea leaves
And their unpredictable presentiments,
Wheresoever with recognitions dim and faint.
Each inscrutable utterance defies our struggle
To find the elusive referent, the obscured mystical link,
Blurred within that hazened purlieu of unconscious perpendings,
Concealed and subsumed amongst warrens of lost thought.

2

We walk occult paths of standing miracles,
As wild and diverse as the wanton winds,
Paths too harrowing to face in waking life, freighted with danger,
As the appertaining wheel grinds that grist which fear cannot,
While eyes are wide awake.
Without reservation, we dive into dark pools
Of absurdity absolute and inchoate comprehensions,
Wherefore we cannot say,
Plunged into an obscure reservoir of knowing and unknowing,
Well immersed into the crazy currents unquestioned.
Ancient injuries, buried inly long ago,
Stubbornly bubble to the surface, swimming into sight,
Recondite rivulets seeking spiritual anodynes of resolution;

Yet unmet aspirations somehow blossom on the tree.
We are appareled in foreign fabrics, seemingly tactile,
Textiles woven of dissociated threads and unfamiliar filaments,
Borne of obscure feelings, awakening singular things forgotten,
Things which lie beyond our ken.
As the tapers yet burn through that elusive night,
We are presented with chimerical koans and perplexing paradoxes,
Compelled to conjoin the incongruous,
Disparate and dispersed, as a shifting sheet of sand;
As tortillons gently blend ambiguous tints,
Chains of reverie are held together by flimsy, fortuitous links,
As to endeavor to hold water in a sieve.

3

Odd goblins lie just beyond our grasp!
Vague visions somehow elude us—
Furtively darting, as minnows in the shallows,
As a deliberate parade of particles,
Coruscating corpuscles of light, bright isotopes,
Tied together like gyrating kite tails in winnowing winds,
As though barefoot whirling dervishes, spinning in search of enlightenment,
All celebrating newfound chaos and novelty,
Yet somehow visionary and portentous—
Such are the atoms of dreams.

HAUNTINGS

In the days when obscure phantasms were inscrutable,
I once inhabited a porch with ceilings painted in haint blue,
While my exigent hauntings eluded exegesis.
At that time, I fell into a singular dappled dream,
A fantastical ague passing through the straits of fear—
Call it a nightmare—
When I was wrested away by faint wraiths,
Amidst exotic strains of psaltery and sung canticles,
As though steeped in vapors of absinthe,
So crystallized, so complete;
It pretty much confirmed everything.
But in time such specters would be absorbed,
Dispelled and dispersed, as if into my morning coffee.

A CHANCE ENCOUNTER

We'd been so close, our friendship did so thrive;
Some time had passed since last I'd seen him alive.
One night, I chanced to meet him in a dream;
His presence was as real as it could seem.

As concrete as the day, this dream did feel;
I tremulously asked him, "Is this real?".
He answered me with patent calm assurance,
"Yes, it is"— no fantastical occurrence.

"It's great to see you", replying as I dared,
"But I must confess, I'm just a little scared."
With a peaceful glow that, in life, we just don't see,
He smiled and simply answered me, "Don't be."

WHILE SLEEPING

While sleeping, so I shed a tear;
She comes to me faint, as a wraith.
I slumber as an act of faith:
In dreams, she will appear.

Her kind embrace is my delight—
Such congress, I would not forsake;
She visits me till I awake,
When day brings back my night.

MAGIC

1

Some are aspiring mathematical mystics,
As if to endeavor to decipher ancient runes;
Some imagine magic to be
The province of conjurors, astrologers, alchemists, and suchlike.

But the lightsome windows of wonderment are the innocent eyes of children,
Opening their seraphic view to an innumerable company of angels,
To notice the unnoticed magnificences of everyday life.
Some secret truths, concealed from the haughty and erudite,
Are to children readily revealed (who knows how?),
Sweet riddles of lovingkindness haloed with beatific souls.
As the morning star rises in their hearts,
They witness the invisible items of infinitely greater moment,
Miracles which leap out of the ordinary,
Embracing the purity which lies beyond their ken,
As bold as a cacophony of birdcalls at first light,
As though heralded by a fanfare of violins and hautboys,
Yet as subtle as the quiet brightness of blossoming wildflowers.
They inhabit an elfin world, a sundered realm
Which illuminates singular mysteries seen and unseen,
Transported by a mighty escapement of gentle agency
Into the perfect innocence of dreams.
They shed the weary cloak of worry in the buoyancy of joyance,
Like a sonnet adrift in reverie, a timeless poesy;
They are as flickering lights of distant astral torches,
As jocund pursuits in dimlit glades and gardens, starred with fairy lamps.

2

They are steeped in nuance, as an artist's soft painting,
While others live in a fervorless world akin to an architect's drawing,
With thin hard lines of punctilio, leaving no room for ambiguity,
Convinced that the answers to all questions are manifest,
As though laid down through the immutable laws of physics.
Nature plays the flute for them, but they do not dance;
A light shines in the darkness, yet the darkness does not comprehend it;
They look upon the world with archetypal eye service.
Those who cannot see magic do not know
That the wind blows where it wishes,
Yet it cannot be told where it comes from, or where it goes.

Those who know don't say; those who say don't know.

140

GOOD FIRE

It is no witchcraft, but by reason of love,
On my soul there is no other enchantment;
I pray you thus to bewitch and bewitch again,
To have good fire without smoke.

SERVE THEM STILL

They all knew well the art of the old dance;
The spell which the bee-master performed,
When ere he swarmed his bees,
As ancient peasants muttered incantations
To make their fields fertile;
Denizens of a remote seacoast
Searched in hopes of encountering a silkie,
As distant wizards reverenced some twisted tree
About which hung old stories unforgotten.
So are the lessons from the fables of yore,
Grasping them from the brilliant light of Time,
Consigned to age-old rustic superstitions;
Let old spells learned from their ancestors
Serve them still.

MANDALA

From nothing comes nothing;
Nature's sagacity grasps life in the present,
For neither the bear nor the elk frets about the future.

Monks decant cannisters of varicolored sand,
Forming careful geometric lines,
Bright patterns, intricate and deliberate,
A fleeting monument, all to enchant,
Only then to be abruptly dashed into a river.

For the greatest monument to impermanence
Is no monument at all.

APPARITION

Weary of enduring untold antagonisms,
I sought sleep after toil, port after stormy seas;
Despite all my travails, I was still standing.
Erelong came her unexpected apparition,
Her placid countenance;
Her perfect asymmetries, I wholly embraced.
With thirsts further whetted, but as yet unslaked,
I ventured forth from my constructed redoubt;
Perforce I became transfixed at once,
Fain to receive her kind attention.
Her peerless presence held incomparable cards;
Her soul's embouchure had perfect pitch,
As she smiled at me with blazing, blessed eyes.

ESCAPEMENT

I once escaped escapement itself,
Unreservedly welcomed by a welcoming world,
Where the wild birds take flight and find the sun.
There I was surrounded by the smiling countryside,
Regarding new apparitions for the very first time,
As rare as when the mule foals,
Yet somehow familiar.
Untold acres of tillage and wood sprawled before me,
As cascading white waterfalls cut deep gorges
Through ancient courses of granite.
Traversing the wooded hollow,
I immersed myself baptismal into the cold creek,
Where eroded roots of clinging trees lined the banks.
Amidst the scent of rising woodsmoke of nearby homesteads,
I later betook myself inside at twilight;
Against the door was a goodly branch of rosemary,
Hung about with silken ribbons of all colors.
I was away, yet I was home,
Somehow returning from before,
But when or how, I could not tell.

QUEEN OF STONE

Set the talisman, spread the cards across the table;
In sortilege, the tarot deck reveals the Queen of Stone.
She is a personage marked by propriety—
Unattainable, distant, stoic, rigid, controlled;
She is impervious to verve and of calcified valence,
Situated afar in a remote personmilieu;
Order itself orders the day.
While love is buried beneath a sea of schedules,
Threats are averted, conversion thwarted,
As a coast without harbor, an isle without ardor.
The heart cedes its sway, trying to escape,
But it cannot;
It is bound by battlemented castle walls,
Set with immovable parapets.

THE TEMPLE STAIRCASE

Upon my gleaning, as Ruth in the barley-fields,
Once I got lost inside a sculpture of a temple,
A round, pillared miniature with a staircase inside,
Leading to a dark, mysterious unknown.
In the sculptor's studio, I saw proofs and castings,
Marvelous maquettes,
Showing the sedulous evolution of the work,
A surreal simulacrum,
Yet they revealed nothing of its guarded mystery—
The beckoning, the beyond.
I imagined myself somehow subsumed,
Also in miniature— I know not how—
Walking that temple staircase nothing loath, in chimera,
Faring my way inside that fane to the unfathomed,
Would that I were somehow able to meet my Maker,
Mysterious and unknowable, yet plainly known.
Plying my beads, I thought, "This is strange, I trow".
By what elusive alchemy did shine an enigmatic light,
To illumine bright that unknown space?
By what odd fortune do some approach death,

But to get a brief glimpse of that which is beyond,
Only to be summoned to return, to inform the rest of us?
My tremulous trek on that temple staircase
Remained inscrutable, yet curiously comforting,
As a gentle Voice assured me not to fear my steps,
Welcoming me into the kind mysterious peace
Of His unknown.

Was it a vision, or a waking dream?

OVER MY HEAD

Words fail, as sometimes they should,
For silence is often the most eloquent response;
Sometimes I practice the art of doing nothing,
To see what is there.
Sometimes I write over my head,
As though I were simply watching my hand writing,
Bearing witness to the pen gliding across the paper,
Writing things which lie beyond my most earnest ken.
When later I read the words, they are flashes of silent lightning;
I am not certain what they mean.
I am blessed in such times to be a reckless conjuror,
To conceive things which are over my head,
Remaining unsure of the source,
Perhaps generous integrations from Heaven,
Perchance by high imagination forecast.

WINDLESS

Who heard not what the thunder said?

Restless, our mind is; the wind is no wilder.
Our thoughts are dipping like kites to every current of distraction.
Amidst the adjournment of drowsiness and sleep,
We are adjured to explore fruitful frontiers,
Praying to find that peace which passes understanding.

With earnest diligence and numinous humility,
We are enjoined to penetrate the innermost redoubts,
To access the quiescent shelter of deep-lying zones,
Places where no human tongue shall utter words,
Muted in resplendent silence.
A cleansing, coughing wind soughs through the trees,
Yet we pray to quell the whispering, victorious breath.
We retreat from the world's mundane panorama,
Prodding against the prosaic, blotting the clatter,
Shielding our ears from the filching lilt of lutes and cymbals,
Averting our eyes from the gyre of wildly-spinning whirligigs;
For the light of a lamp does not flicker in a windless place.

TWO MONKS

Two monks traversed a mountain path,
One young, and his master old;
Their great ascent afforded them
A world at their feet to behold.

Great plains and valleys lie below,
Long rivers ran to the sea;
The old monk sat in meditation;
Content to pray softly, was he.

The young monk cried, "How beautiful!",
As he found that he needed to pray so;
The old monk smiled and simply replied,
"What a pity to have to say so."

LET OLD THINGS PASS

Let old things pass;
Shed past prolusions,
As though discarding an affixed frontispiece to a commonplace book;
Surrender consternations,
When the strangling clinging stifles the now in the hoary frost of ago.

So I heeded these words, proceeding apace, eliding silently,
Bound for amelioration, albeit not glory,
Sheltered alee from the winds of pure fury.
I soon drifted off to sleep in dimming lanternlight,
Entering a singular dreamscape;
There I beheld saturnine souls
Who solaced themselves as they spoke in sundry tongues,
Eluding grim reminders of guilt,
As the ghost of Banquo[21], as a jailbird in the window,
As drear soaring kites seeking the carrion below;
Whereupon I saw the futility of all this,
Recasting lost hopes from the seedbed of disillusionment.
And so I was delivered from past disturbances,
Girded against pelting hailstorms from frozen clouds high above,
Comforted by the certainty of awaiting calmer provinces,
Placidly letting old things pass.

WELTSCHMERZ[22]

The skies summoned thunder and its elemental spirits,
Confronting the ice with force through mystical affinity,
Jostling princes on the pavements;
Beneath the canopy of great empires,
Coolness and skill fell to alarm and abnegation,
Amidst the potent hold of sorry caricatures,
Narrow and peculiar, in ponderous facades;
Some gathered as 'round the bed of a sick man,
In varying guise of vulture or physician.
Yet the timeless hegemony of Heaven
Has thwarted the *Weltschmerz* of vile detractors,
In quest of *revanche* of something lost, something numinous,
Holding at bay melancholy and soporific decay;
The sought salvation from a more powerful Sun
Has illuminated the mysterious inner spaces,
Casting altogether welcome lights and shadows.

---

[21] See Shakespeare, *Macbeth*
[22] A feeling of melancholy and world-weariness

XII.   Meditations

THE PURE LIGHT

Consider me pardonably confused;
The times of luxuriant blooming are now passed.
In the midst of a day of promise, something like a calamity befell it;
Just when all seemed well, I saw still another portent,
Looming events with certain marked peculiarities.
Legions of aspirants genuflect in sad gestures of blind obeisance to craven idols,
Trading their honor and reputations as cheap chattel,
Brandishing tongues sharper than any cutlass,
While casting scrofulous shadows of reproof on the innocent.
Serfs are now habituated to a penurious tenantry,
Induced to come to the sad defense of their chains,
Yoking themselves to doctrinaire sacrosanct axioms,
Beholden to tsars of paper-credit empires,
Whence there are no small number of charlatans,
Mountebanks with pretensions hardly concealing their true sympathies,
As tares among the wheat,
In the main fraught with fraud and peculation.
Each age upends the extant certitudes of science,
Somehow daring to imagine even greater marvels;
And so now I see a world at present,
Daring to upend its own unyielding laws of material conceptions.
What is now left is something less tangible, something bordering on mystery—
A world which endeavors to return
To an unadulterated realm of our ancestral ghosts,
The Pure Light by which all things are measured and treasured.

DREAMS UNFULFILLED

A child's heart is broken by misfortunes we think trivial—
A broken doll, a lost toy—
Yet how much are we like that child!
May we ever see the blessings of dreams unfulfilled;
For too often, once we get there,
All is not what we imagined it to be.
In vanity, racing faster and faster for less and less,
We reach the pinnacles that do not bring the joy expected;
We play the game capably, yet find the laurels inadequate.

Where is the glory of the dream?
Bold clarions of promise fade into diminished, inarticulate whispers.
Worldly things, once worn out, lie exposed and vitiated,
Leaving us the wisdom to seek more durable things,
To draw from the deep cistern—
To draw from it unceasingly,
Seeking the Eternal, hidden, and incomprehensible Peace,
Like a bird flying beatific through innumerable clouds,
Confident to reach the Light.

WHITHER ARE WE BOUND? (I)

Whither are we bound?
Where shall we rest tonight?
What will we have found?

May we survive to see our sorrow drowned?
Shall we endure this weary, worthy fight?
Whither are we bound?

How tightly must our tethers still be wound?
Shall we ever see the end of this sad plight?
What will we have found?

How many steps to sanctuary ground?
How long must we so strive with all our might?
Whither are we bound?

May we finally hear that waiting, welcome sound?
Is our distant destination yet in sight?
What will we have found?

How long must our patient cries resound?
May we leave at first light?
Whither are we bound?
What will we have found?

WHITHER ARE WE BOUND? (II)

Whither are we bound?
Leaving sere deserts of lands once fair,
Embracing visions fragmentary yet illuminating,
Our subsumed hopes for the expiry of the fury
Lay in the realm of pious wishes;
Yet whereas the seas of reason have receded,
Nonetheless the waters serve to extinguish vile flames.
We stare at each other, strangers as we are,
Suddenly sure that, after all, somehow we are kin,
Somehow soldered together by our consanguinity;
I know who you are, even though I do not know your name.
Where shall we rest tonight?
We do not know.
Whither are we bound?

LIFE CYCLES

We are as an enigmatic palimpsest,
A penned manuscript, effaced, erased, appended, and evolved,
Re-engraved, yet still bearing traces of our earlier form;
Our past still bleeds through the parchment,
Despite redemption and reinvention;
New writing supplants strange elisions of prior experience,
Embracing the architecture of renewal and repair.
Life cycles as it moves forward, repeating as it is redefined,
As a borrowed pastiche of our past iterations,
Setting to scale insuperable mountains, as gravity exerts it inexorable sway
Against the most ambitious leaps and laudatory climbs.
Indeed the highest redwood boughs
Owe their outstretched majesty to their sprawling roots far below;
New branches of life shoot forth after the windthrown tree has fallen,
Bright scions nourished by the abiding secret roots underground.
As we are constantly humbled in the face of our most lofty ascents,
There is no cause for shame or diminishment,
For it is a circle, and not a straight line:
We are today what we were yesterday.

SHADOWS

My obligations are legion; I have quarried from innumerable sources.
I navigate staccato tests of strength, parrying with sanctimonious souls,
Sordid satraps who turn their backs in supercilious poses.
They transgress the limits of elementary prudence,
Failing to see the folly of human aspirations to match primal forces.
They make perfunctory pious affirmations, where zeal outstrips knowledge,
Supposititious as they gallop gaily into untenable positions,
To the despair of soberer comrades who go their wonted way;
They exult in songs of unbridled hubris,
While the saint and the prophet hear them with tears.
I seek refuge in the palladiums of promise,
In the harbors of welcome harbingers;
I recall conversations once audible to awestruck valiant hearts,
Auspicious incipiencies of the ages that are now gone.
These are but past palavers once held in sunshine and soft tones,
Only to surrender to the surge of thunder and storm.
I now encounter a whirling eddy in merging streams,
Mere shadows of the house where I once dwelt;
Whereupon the lamp which once cast long rays
Has been dimmed by the smoke of tabescence.

STRATA

1

In the fullness of faith, bold and ebullient,
While walking along a remote path,
I saw rocks of gneiss, schist, and feldspar,
In muted blacks, whites, grays, and reds,
Each bearing coarse and variegated markings,
Lineaments of igneous and metamorphic origin,
Formed through an infinity of epochs.
Although I knew not their names,
I had seen and known these rocks all along;
All of these were as though retained
Through some strange geologic morphology,
Obscured in coterminous synclines and anticlines,
So deeply embedded in the earth as to seem antipodal.

154

I ruminate as to the origin of these rocks which lie across my path.
They are borne of ancient volcanic pressures,
Primordial forces seeking exothermic expression
Through annealing cauldrons of shifting tectonics,
Inscrutable lodes beckoning to be explored and extracted,
As are the interstices of human mysteries, somehow known,
And yet abstruse and still to be revealed—
Thousands of glimpses forgotten,
Memories ephemeral, dismissed through time,
Yet remaining as treasured untold latencies.
The effulgence illuminates marked yet elusive paths,
Originating from timeless subterranean strata of unknown provenance,
Abysses not altogether fathomed.

SILKSCREEN

We behold the fleeting present as though through warped panes of glass,
Perspectives lost in the blur of contemporary whir,
When superstition becomes the conjecture of fire-eating orators,
And then conjecture becomes the inevitable, with certitudes shaken.
Through clearer panes, we later decipher past riddles and runes,
Grandiloquent words now read easily,
Appearing apposite through the wondrous temporal silkscreen,
As with a painter who paints pictures defying ordinary eyes.

THE PILOT LIGHT

I celebrate the bright flame when we are together,
And I remain steadfast through dim light when we are apart,
Separated but not separate.
Amidst the sundered siege of my sorry absence,
Resisting the flickers of flame in a world mutable,
I maintain resolve of our love through the persistence of the steady pilot light,

That faithful scion of flame which suspires in quiet constancy.
Such an unassuming scintilla of humble luminescence
Is nonetheless fueled inexhaustibly by the hope of my return,
Conveying me through darkness when ardent desires are sublimated,
Awaiting patiently for the time when these have culminated
Into restoration of our bright flame when we have reunited,
All kept faithfully alive by the pure, steady pilot light.

RETURN

1

Speak, Memory!

I yearn in earnest discernment of recondite reckonings.
In the midst of cold winter, I am given to hibernal dreams,
Wonderful to relate, vast, supple, and subtle.
I clamber forth into crowded linen closets bearing buoyant clues,
As faded footprints on a forgotten terrain,
Or as a sphinxlike riddle, eluding comprehension, yet ever more impelling.
As the squirrel fills its granary in the fall for access in winter,
I ferret out remote fossils of summer,
Appertaining artifacts which have long outlived their eclipse—
Awake and open the quiescent sluices of memory and imagination!
Embedded in the fabric of folded beach towels
Are the faint scents of sea salt and aloe: Breathe it in!
Forgotten fragrances summon sweet images
Of grassy sand dunes and crashing blue surf,
Golden olfactory glimpses, at once elusive and ephemeral,
All fleeting like an evanescent adolescence—
Enlist the senses, refind them all!

2

Would that I could be there now!
These are all vanished estival aspirations,
Save as abstraction, solemn and secret, as stray dormant seeds,
Drowsily asleep under the deep white snowy expanse,
Silently awaiting the certainty of their germination,

As sanguine sproutings of an exotic cultivation.
All are buried notions now furnishing to embryo,
Sensations strangely hidden, yet perdurable, bestirred mightily,
More accessible than through the most eloquent disquisition.
I am happily lost in a world seven walls away,
Dominated by scions of wonder and affection;
In a dreamy mood emanating from romantic sources,
As rare music of unusual scales and mystical dissonances,
I endeavor to recapture visions of precarious tenancy.
These are inhabited by a general and generous desire,
An accession to a trail of lost reveries,
As the discovery of ancient epochal texts,
The renascence of forgotten remembrances.
Wherefore the elements and structure are safely hidden,
Quite secure and well-nigh complete,
Surely hopeful for yet another return.

PLACE THE LAMP HIGH

Place the lamp high, illuminate the room,
Cast light on those misfortunes which may loom;
Withstand the forces fraught with dark derision;
Fail not to seek a clarity of vision.

Some tarnish lamps of high imagination;
They shroud their light with veils of derogation.
They obfuscate the fates which might befall—
Those windmills, they were giants, after all.

THE TREE MOST SHAKEN

In orchards true, there is a tree,
Whence the fruit is taken;
The tree which bears abundant fruit,
The tree most strongly shaken.

Its trunk must bear the hardest strains,
Its branches know not how;
When much is given, give we must,
So droops the bowing bough.

The hungry seek the richest tree,
They seek its sagging load;
Heaven inheres in heartwood strong,
When blessings are bestowed.

THINGS HARMLESS

In the small hours of the morning,
I was absorbed in ruminations on the nature of fear,
Lost in luminous lucubrations;
After spending much ink, yet a bit somnolent,
I ventured out for a ride on horseback through an arid desertscape.
A hot foehn wind arose, sending some tumbleweed across my path,
Harmless enough, or so I thought,
Until the strange rolling masses discountenanced my mount,
Its hooves struggling for purchase on its path;
My horse panicked, almost bucking me, as I narrowly averted a calamity.
All wherewith my nocturnal perpendings were rendered clear;
Such things which seem benign, while their danger lies obscured—
I fear things harmless for the harm that they can do.

LOOSED REINS

A wise equestrian counseled me
As to when to loosen the reins;
He gave me this sage instruction,
As my horse approached rocky terrains.

I loosened the reins as I noticed
A steep ledge at the side of the trail,
Permitting my mount to look downward,
Selecting its steps without fail.

And so I learned a great lesson,
A tenet to guide my life as a whole:
The lesson of learning to loosen the reins,
The wisdom of ceding control.

CHRYSALIS

We yearn to unfetter from a frozen tundra,
Caught in a whorl of cautious, cold isolation,
Spurned by stubborn fears of the prevalent malaise;
Molting by inches, proceeding sparingly, in sustained solitude,
We seek to flex circumspect wings, in hopes to elude the persistent frost.
Yet foul gravity exerts its inexorable pull,
As a perplexed weaver might conjoin dissociated strands of fibers.
Desperate for the forgotten tonic of human interplay,
It is as though we abandon a comforting warm poultice—
But is it safe to come out yet?

CANYONLANDS

My soul is like a runaway horse,
Seeking refuge from the torrents scourging the plains,
Yet also seeking to behold the torrents unfettered,
Making way with wanton gallops,
Far removed from a foal's first timid missteps,
Venturing into the dark, illuminating spaces
I call Canyonlands.

To mine the treasures of the heart, I shun safe caverns,
In deference to dangerous curiosities;
I ply the cliff-edges of Vision,
Searching layers of dark canyons for perilous, priceless pearls,
Hurtling beyond Reason and Fear,
Into the feral free-for-all and the full-tilt gestalt.

But sometimes I get wounded,
Bringing back the beauty from these Canyonlands.

LINGUA FRANCA

Some are speaking words inscrutable,
Like some remote patois,
An indistinct *quechua*, a lost linguistics,
A fleeting philology with faded phonetics;
Their speech bears no alphabet, no orthography,
As some long-forgotten, undeciphered rune.
Theirs are hidden conversations, cryptic idioms and cognate collocations,
Spoken with strange accents, like mumbled palavers between mute mystics;
As practitioners of obscure mother tongues,
These are speakers talkative or taciturn, as moods change;
Theirs is misspent eloquence, never to reach its intended destination,
Yet sometimes denominated as genius.

THE UNCOMMON SHIFT

Caught in this self-drawn, late-night light,
And in this time of my unconscious picking,
I find myself on the uncommon shift,
Working to see myself ticking.

So strange it is, to think these thoughts,
And to think about the one who is thinking;
For in a sea of roles and worldly affairs,
I forget that I am constantly sinking.

COLORED SCREENS

I stood outside two colored screens,
You stood inside, in-between;
One screen yellow, the other blue,
We saw differently, me and you.

You saw me as yellow, you saw me as blue,
Depending on where I stood from you;
And the same for me as it was for you,
You were sometimes yellow, and sometimes blue.

We were both right and we were both wrong;
Colors continue, and backgrounds prolong.
And sometimes we saw each other as green—
But let us not dwell upon colored screens.

EUROPA

The ancients named their ancient places,
Following the path of the sun, moving westward:
Asia is where the sun rises,
And Europa is where the sun sets.
Our world is consonant with where we sit to regard it.

A mother sits with her child by a tree,
Seeking safety during an earthquake.
Days later, the child points to the tree:
"That is where the earthquake happened."

PAREIDOLIA

As a child, I might have been seven,
I lay in the grass, I lay on my back;
I gazed up to the province of heaven,
To see in the clouds a face staring back.

I kept seeing faces as I got older,
In ridges of rock, I saw those *visages*;
And then from the moon came gapes even bolder,
Those lunar faces were hardly mirages.

In slabs of marble, in panels of wood,
The faces all gazed from a terrace;
I thought to tell others, but I never could,
Uncertain, and feeling embarrassed.

To be a child again, ever so free,
Serene and without a care;
Then it all plainly occurred to me—
Who can't see faces everywhere?

VALEDICTION

They said goodbye without saying goodbye;
Their cleaving left a deckled edge,
As they left a billion bits of experience,
All fractionated beyond recognition,
As stippling on the substrate;
There was so much *denouement* left,
The deafening roar of things left unsaid.
And their eyes conveyed their unspoken valediction:
"I see your faces, and I hear your voices."

YELLOW LINES

I once sought escapement from escalating melancholy,
Taking to the refuge of distant roads,
Transported by precarious conveyances.
Imagining such highways would render deliverance,
I traveled until I reached the most remote stations,
Only discover that trouble also travels that elusive tarred thoroughfare,
Stubbornly following me wherever I went,
Tethered tenacious to the yellow lines.

ROMANCE

For every journey glorified,
For every story's turn,
We seek the skillful alchemist—
The dreamer does return.

So thus the essence molds and bakes,
For present clay is commonplace;
And is it loss or is it gain,
When time does glaze and paint the face?

CALLUSES

Laboring in the scorching hot tobacco fields,
I spent my teenage summers building calluses on my hands,
Subjected to the imprecations of martinets.
Each day in the fields, as I picked tobacco leaves,
My hands were encrusted corrosive,
With greenish-black grime and layers of DDT;
But the poison and grime never seeped through my calluses.

Years later, I traded all this for a briefcase,
Erelong exchanging exhaustion and tired muscles
For flights of nightmares and lost sleep,
Missing the simplicity of unencumbered slumber;
Corrosive worry was the price I had paid.
But I somehow steeled myself against all this—
The poison and grime still never seeped through my calluses.

WHAT THE ORCHARD BEARS

Unreasoning arrogance often attends high prosperity,
In the misplaced milieu where money supplants the sacred manna,
Where is paid sad obeisance to the deity of the dollar sign,
Where the voices of righteous angels are muted and occluded.
In the allure of worldly cities made by hands,
It falls to the lot of the few to fructify in fortune and yet remain free of pride,
Eschewing the wizards and conjurors of earthly ways;
For the orchard bears the labor of its fruit.

LESS OF A LOSS

'Tis a sad misfortune like no other brings,
Mourning mighty contests of trivial things;
Daft recriminations must so cease,
To crown the journey from malaise to peace.

To the futile exercise of second-guessing,
A fleeting memory is indeed a blessing;
To grasp this one truth erases the pain:
Less of a loss is a gain.

IF THEY KNEW

In the face of challenges near and dire,
We access the fuel of our dreams;
The stumbles we face along the way
Make attainment more faint than it seems.

We aspire to stand on the shoulders of giants—
If only we could have *been* more;
Nobody would ever do anything,
If they knew what they were in for.

MY FAVORITE NOTEBOOK

Scribblings of scattered thoughts,
Bound together by rings of steel,
Forged into paper, forced back to memory,
To remember as I ought.
But if I had but one to choose,
I would choose my favorite notebook;
That which gathers the scatterings, without rings of steel,
That which forges into pages not of paper;
And if I had but one to choose,
I would choose my favorite notebook.

WORLDS OF FANCIES

Beauty obscures the danger held by a haughty heart,
With speaking looks that hidden glances bear.
With walls so strong, yet that constant battery did rive,
His message got swallowed by a sea of competing voices,
Drowned by sacraments profane.
And so to sea he did repair, luffing up into strong headwinds,
Consigned to saline nothingness, where long he was led many years,
Wandering from shore to shore, as a pilgrim seeking far-off shrines,
Ably charting many reefs on which the unwary might make shipwreck,
Amidst riddles devised, ere rest he found.
Indeed he traveled (if I remember right) through weary wars and labors long,
Fashioning worlds of fancies evermore.

FORGOTTEN WONDERS

Immersed sedulous in the visitation of a whorldream,
Fervently focused, as if praying in an oratory,
I greet redolent moments of indiscernible beauty,
When feet tap to the elusive thrum of that once-familiar tabor drum,
Suffused with far-heard textured tones, as vague strains of distant clarinets.
I am happily reacquainted with recondite recollections,
Things once lost which are now somehow manifest,
As brushes beckoned to the hues of hidden palettes,
As alluring patterns of remote damasked fabrics,
As a granting goddess whose bright eyes rain influence from the skies,
All with the splendid uncertainty of certain forgotten wonders.

TOO MUCH ANALYSIS

The eyes of cold intellect blur the pure light;
They mute all the beauty and kill all delight.
Harsh alkaline minds render so much paralysis:
Truth suffers from too much analysis.

EN SOI, POUR SOI[23]

While navigating the perilous waters of protean seas,
Plying the giant waves of Hokusai[24],
We reckon our bearings and set course by our lodestar,
Tacking hard with taut sails toward journey's end;
By indirections, we find directions out.
As we cross turbulent narrows,
Twin hazards flank the channel in augury of menace,
As though Scylla and Charybdis[25].
We seek enticing currents awaiting on the other side,
But first we confront a precarious choice:
To remain in the treacherous safety of stagnant, want-begotten waters,
Or to venture in gyre through the dangerous maelstrom,
In order to achieve ambitious aims.
As we sail through that ineluctable strait, so we must decide:
To be in ourselves, or for ourselves—
Or would that we could be both.

THE ARBOR SECCO[26]

"I see the *Arbor Secco*",
These ancient words I read;
In a tale of his Eastern sojourn,
So the Western traveler said.

Such a sole tree, he did espy,
In the midst of a desert expanse;
For this singular tree, green and thriving,
Must have made his Venetian eyes dance.

And so it is with we travelers,
Who subsist in the stark and the sere;
We likewise so compass our journey,
As through the vast desert, we dare.

---

[23] "In oneself, for oneself"; from an ontological essay by Sartre
[24] Nineteenth-century Japanese artist
[25] Mythical sea monsters described by Homer in *The Odyssey*
[26] "The dry tree"; from *The Travels of Marco Polo*

LEISURE

There is no harder work than idleness,
Hunting everywhere for what cannot be found;
In the search for rest and fulfillment,
The wayward fates of sloth will confound.
We yearn for the blessing of kind repose,
At a time when we truly need it;
Strange torment, to seek the comfort of leisure,
Without the toil and fatigue which must precede it.

XIII.   Of God and Spirituality

ANCIENT OF DAYS

1

What happens when the falcon no longer heeds the falconer?
We are as fragile blossoms afloat on a torrent.
Many are confused by the plethora of illusive lodestars,
Mesmerized by the unfolding folderol.
They plot foolish courses with a fouled compass,
Following a false magnetic north, an addled azimuth;
They are spellbound by the seductive sighs of sibyls and augurs,
Rending the skies with their loud applause;
They treasure those worldly hopes that turn to ashes,
Ephemeral meadows that bloom and wither,
All the while ignoring the simple humble truths.
They seek the sorry counsel of romancers and necromancers,
As they eschew the beloved for the bedeviled,
Mere human contrivances that vanish in a dream,
As a bat retreats in a panic moment upon close of night
And the onset of first light.

2

But the wise shed the trance they are under,
Rejecting a sad collusion of foolish elements,
Abandoning the folly of striving to confute the light;
They track the true star of divine light in the sky,
Setting their course through a worthy magnetic lodestone.
They surrender their blindness,
With the shifting of wonder and the transference of awe,
To honor the Ancient of Days
Who bestows on us the purest of pure kindness.
With the solid certitude of timeless truths beyond peradventure,
With the simple acceptance of a child,
The riddles of the universe become unraveled and revealed,
Defying the ageless consternation of theologians and mystics;
Thrilling theophanies surround us every day, but to have to look!
For the wonder of that which is seen
Opens our eyes to that which is unseen.

PARTICLE

Of what avail are erudition and eloquence, without simple wisdom?
What is the measure of my worth if I say foolish things?
Who am I but a minute particle of the whole?

I am but a fleeting footnote in the expanse of the human story;
I am smaller than the minutest atom,
A humble scintilla in the scheme of God's creation.
Each microscopic movement in each cell of my body,
Each one of millions of recondite mitoses,
Each molecule of myriad chemical forces inside of me—
All of this has been carefully ordained by Heaven.
Wherefore each step I have taken, each word I have spoken,
Each thought, each idea I have ever had,
All has been a gift from God.
Every word I write, indeed even the simple power to grasp this pen,
Cannot be done without His blessing, His grace.
Each stroke of my paintbrush, each musical note my fingers play,
Each melody I invent— but I have invented nothing!
I pour my words in humble supplication for Heaven's blessings;
It is He who permits me to see and hear,
Even to possess the clarity of my mind's eye.
The proud man boasts, "Look what I have done!";
Professing to be wise, he becomes a fool;
He is a cloud without water, carried about by the winds.
For which one of us has not given a gift to another,
Only to be disappointed by the ingratitude of the recipient?
And so I strive to be thankful in humility,
To be a worthy recipient of His grace.
Let the virgin lamps ever be filled with oil,
To shed His wondrous light.

DELIVERANCE

Once trapped in a maze, I saw no way out;
My own missteps, I now had to pay for.
I was deeply steeped in confusion—
I didn't even know what to pray for.

172

So I simply prayed for His deliverance,
And I trusted Him to handle the rest;
Then He took care of everything—
When we pray in that way, it is best.

THE WAY

Out of the transitory smoke of all human glory, we search for The Way.
In the search for Truth, the road is manifold and the paths various.
Wayfarers approach from diverse directions,
Each by his own winding thoroughfare;
But the sinuous passageways converge and coalesce,
As if the oceans had sprinkled them into a single pool.
Sky and earth, winds, sea, and clouds are given to all in common;
The just and unjust live under a single sky;
The pious and impious breathe the same air;
Yet as clear as the night from the day, as the mute from the articulate,
All paths lead to a single path,
The path to The Way.

THE CHAPEL

Surpliced figures are seated in devotion,
As soft illumination leaks through the leaded panes.
Many in the chapel silently pray to retain the holy,
Holding onto the wisdom to mold oneself to the spiritual,
And not the spiritual to oneself,
The purity which underlies true worship.
But others pursue a different path;
They are assiduous in prayer, more of habit than conviction,
Eyeing the clock in perfunctory adoration,
Welded into the refuge of superficial rituals;
They recite by rote prayers of particular monotony,
Hurried through with scant devotion,
Mouthing half-hearted orisons, gabbling slurred paternosters,
Mumbling hasty vespers, and breezing through the briefest of brevaries.

With generous allusions to the maxims of saints,
They navigate through foggy swamps
Of incense emanating from chain-swung censers,
Awash with ablutions and surrounded by statuary,
Against a multitude of haloed images and mechanical routines.
They are reassured by the comfort of hieratic gestures,
Figures arrayed in bright brocaded and embroidered vestments,
With arms raised.

HAPPENSTANCE

I am commended never to overlook happenstance,
Nor to relegate unexpected blessings to the sorry province of coincidence;
There is nothing coincidental about a blessing,
Nothing accidental about a gift from God.
Divine magic is never random, never stochastic;
Such things do not happen without reason.
Here manifests a world constantly mutable,
With unimagined blessings flowing in flux,
Always arriving and ever becoming, ever in everlasting change,
As though swingling raw flax to become fine linen;
It is a plea answered, a gift not to be questioned.
I am in love with all of these blessings, individually and severally;
They sustain me, as they sustain themselves.
In this joyous, enigmatic whorl, I am wholly and irretrievably immersed;
There is no going back.

THE GLAZIER

How shall I describe the wondrous works of Our Lord?
Shall I compare Him to a Master Glazier?
As an Architect of Light, He provides worthy windows
Which permit His kind illumination to enter our abode,
Wherethrough unfiltered rays abet our feeble vision;
He urges that we see past walls otherwise opaque,
Rendering clear an entire world outside of our own;
All the while He barricades the rain and other adverse elements,

Keeping at bay Time and Death, when they would seize us.
As an artist overlays on canvas bright shades of paint against the dark,
As a composer juxtaposes major chords against those of the yin-minor,
So He displays effulgent truths against the obscure torpor.

THE BENEFACTOR

A bird once was trapped indoors, flailing in feathered panic,
Flinging itself against closed panes of glass,
Sad interdictions forbidding flight;
The bird urgently sought escape.
A gentle Personage approached to assist,
Coaxing the confused creature to reach the outside;
The terrified bird did not understand, evading the proffered aid.
The availing Personage gently persisted,
Shepherding the tiny soul through an open passageway,
Abetting the certain sanctuary of its release.
A recipient of kind intercession,
The freed bird remained unaware of its Benefactor,
Happily flying otherwhere.

SOME GREAT THING

We so aspire to do some great thing,
Imagining the joy that it would bring;
But greatness isn't framed in human glory,
Those worldly laurels, worn and transitory.

The dignity of doing some great thing
Is quite within our reach through simple living;
The loving parent who cares for a child,
The laborer who toils in the weather wild.

The nameless holy, so unrecognized,
The unknown saints, none ever canonized;
They needn't merit haloes here on earth;
Our Lord knows all too well of their true worth.

So in our quest for greatness undeterred,
We humbly seek observance of His Word;
To strive our best to serve our blessed King,
Is surely to accomplish some great thing.

EYES

Eyes cannot know a crooked line, unless they have seen a straight line first.
Such eyes have come to know Truth, and so faith is thus rewarded,
Even while sleepwalking through vanished dreams,
Even while taking stock of unmet astral aspirations.
Therein lies the elegant mystery,
The humility found through accepting all outcomes with grace,
Trading the wound for the golden bow, yet while receiving an unexpected gift,
To see the world again through new eyes:
Believe, and it will be shown to you.

THE LIGHT STILL SHINES

What color is the dark?
What informs the shifting shapes of Time?
How is Death defeated by yet another Life?
Of such questions, no answerer am I;
For to answer such questions is a vocation for the saint and the anchorite.
Yet it doesn't take much to tell that story.
As the tailor bastes the stitches till the garment is complete,
God sews the human fabric, abetted by His sacred thread.
Once tongues of fire overcame the weakness
Of three denials and a doubt;
Make clear the path:
The Light still shines when eyes are closed.

HATRED TO LOVE

Insecurity led to humiliation,
Led to resentment and fury,
Led to hatred causing injury,
Led to satisfaction;
Led to prayer and reflection,
Led to remorse and humility,
Led to generosity and sacrifice,
Led to love.

CLIFFS OF FALL

Tall cliffs of fall,
Frightful and unfathomed,
Seemingly unbottomed,
And sheer withal.

Oh troubled mind,
Its perilous places,
Those uncharted spaces,
Darkness unkind.

Hear me, oh Lord,
I pray be my solace,
Pray that I may harness
Feelings abhorred.

Lord, ease my pain,
Send illumination,
Hear my supplication,
Send my soul rain.

THE YIELD

Being of a different cast of mind,
To look at the world through another's eyes
Is to have another world to live in.
Peace is much more than the absence of war;
It is to yearn for understanding,
To enjoy a wider angle of vision,
Silent harvests of the yield of wisdom,
Journeys which thrill on the first encounter,
On a brilliantly lit highway toward God.

VIEW FROM A PLANE

Our view from a plane, from high above,
Is perhaps as Heaven sees us all, with love;
We imagine His view of the boundless skein,
Regarded from on high, from His mighty fane.

Below, the checkered landscapes sprawl,
With countless thousands of souls, withal;
As some, no doubt, gaze up to the sky,
To watch our plane go passing by.

Those thousands below appear humble and small;
Regardless, we still love them all.
Perhaps this is how He considers us so,
As we consider Him now, from here below.

XIV. Of Old Age and Beyond

IN OUR TIME

Long ago, we were just like you,
Believers in eternal youth;
We roamed the world and we stomped the ground,
You can hear the echoes of our sounds.

In our time, in our time,
We were keepers of the bold eternal light;
In our time, in our time,
We were standing tall like trees against the sky.

Now old age has claimed our time,
We've met the days at the end of our climb;
Our light has dimmed what one was there;
Now we sit in Sickness' chair.

In our time, in our time,
We'll be keepers of the bold eternal light;
In our time, in our time,
We'll be standing tall like trees against the sky.

CONCRETIONS

They knew each other for too long
To separate at a time of life
When neither could afford to hunt for a new partner;
Endeavoring to hasten the dilatory thaw of suppressed passions,
Abetted by moonlight strolls through quiet streets,
They resurrected dreams as durable as concretions of stone and marble.

PROPINQUITY

She gazes out her gray window, enisled on a rainy afternoon,
Surveying with placid yet perplexed eyes,
Abiding her patient isolation,
Importuning who-knows-who for God-knows-what,

183

Praying to saint so-and-so.
Immersed in premonitory daydreams,
The raindrops are brooms to her thoughts,
As she sits and regards the world through blurred panes of glass,
Wondering where the years went,
As if the fleeting sheets of water
Which descend at once from the remote heavens
Might collect awash in the purgatory chasm,
Somehow bearing propinquity to her solitary circumstance.

THE PICNIC SPOT

Once long ago, we sojourned there,
On the brightest day of spring;
We picnicked where the grasses grew green,
And the birds did sing.

We shared an unforgotten smile,
In unforgotten light;
A day which time cannot efface,
When hope shown bright.

Such echoes of our picnic past,
Resplendent still in mind;
Alive as though 'twere yesterday,
Remembrances kind.

Yet now she faces final slumber,
Fading somber, now supine;
Lost in thoughts of lasting comfort,
Of love divine.

And now I sojourn there again,
This time, alone and wandering;
Though the grasses have withered in the Autumntide,
And no birds sing.

ONE AUTUMN AFTERNOON

A leaf fell on my lap today,
It chanced to blow my way;
The wind, the time, the place were set;
The leaf had met its day.

I sat beneath a shielding tree,
It wavy, mottled form;
It joined with others, yielding free
Their falling, filling storm.

To see this happen here is odd,
Amidst these granite stones;
To sight the constant pageantry
Each memory intones.

For leaves may be the many,
As the falling, scattered flow;
Or one leaf may be the any,
Separate from the flocks that blow.

It chanced to seem irregular,
That while one leaf did fly,
It would but sit upon my spot
That beckoned it to lie.

Now situations curious
Do often join and share;
For as I viewed one leaf, one stone,
I did perceive a pair.

Beyond the leaf was Harry's bier,
He was a man obscure;
And though he only seems a stone,
He thought these thoughts, I'm sure.

For like their fallen elegies,
These souls, by markers lie;
These stones and leaves uncountable,
These few that pass me by.

They are the same, yet different,
These names and leaves unknown;
Such storming singularities,
Till single leaves are shown.

One soul in time and place unique,
One leaf, one tree, one season;
And why one blows across my path,
I cannot tell the reason.

WITNESS

Listen to the melancholy quietude of a long-forgotten grave,
After the strains of distant dirges and echoes of obsolete obsequies
Faded at once into the inviolable bygone night.
See the recondite granite stone, with weathered lettering,
The sole persistent witness of the congregated mourners long ago,
When a concourse of weeping people followed him to his last rest,
Amidst the plaintive cries of owls and soft, sibilant whispers.
Past tearful lamentations are now supplanted;
Profound paroxysms of grief and ululations are now muted
Through the silent poesy of time.
Perhaps his gentle spirit patiently abides invisible here,
As a reticent wraith, a subtle specter;
Alas, we hear him no longer.
Something of the mellow sadness of an autumn evening ever hangs,
When Beauty and Death went hand in hand,
With a graceful and elegiac sigh.

THE LAST TIME

The shock hit hard when I heard the news—
It was rather unexpected;
Nobody saw that burning fuse;
Its glow went undetected.

I recalled how we had sailed at sea,
In a way only Fate could contrive;
How strange, it then occurred to me,
That was the last time I'd seen him alive.

And so, with friends and time so fleeting,
When do we see them last?
We never know our final meeting,
Until the time has passed.

WHO NEXT?

In quietude of fragile dance,
Pervading scales and songs thereunder,
To know that which transplants,
Sustains itself, constrained to wonder

Where we find the will to weather
Wintry torrents, seeking sage
Abiding shelters, all together,
Walloped by the winds of age.

So I stand with those still standing,
Fortunate to see this day
Of sunlight, at the Lord's commanding,
To be among the ones who stay.

As so depart my friends so fond,
I wonder if I could not seek
A glimpse of what awaits beyond
This earth—if just a passing peek.

That I be granted peace, I pray,
To live in measured peace, not fear
Of reaching my own certain day—
But now, who next will disappear?

OF OLD AGE

1

After a while, maybe becomes no;
Hopes of long duration cannot last in life's brief glimmer.
With the tolling of many a twelvemonth,
So intense and brilliant is the beacon in the gloaming,
The focused light of countless memories.
Yet to retain the grasp of the past proves elusive;
As the glow slowly diffuses, chastened with age,
Fleeting moments are lost in faint, dappled shafts of brittle twilight.
Light after light in the house goes out,
Each against a clamoring bell of quittance and annunciation,
Leaving fewer awake by candleside with fires gone gray.
As eyes grow dim with gazing on fading stars,
We note the silent passing of autumn flowers, lamenting their sad eclipse;
How do we measure the flicker of a mortal human life?
Upon looking back at what had been and might have been,
Some reflect with peaceful satisfaction,
While palsied hearts who once aspired to fulfillment
Pray to fill the cup that clears the day of past regrets;
We are what we have been.

2

Each wave withdraws, each subsiding seaward,
Yet the ebb retains it own beauty in submission,
As with the enduring lineaments of fading countenances,
Adorned by the habiliments of farewell.
Amidst strains of ancient riddle songs,
As a whispered psalm in the night,
Voices fade wayward in valedictory melody,
As that of a swan, suspiring yet expiring,
Facing the inescapable embrace of eternity.
Nonetheless we are hopeful to be assumed heavenward in humble fragility,
Wishing to depart from a temporal house constructed of clay and wattles,
Aspiring to be transported by divine conveyance to a realm of empyreal heights,
Where finite hearts yearn for the promise of infinite love,
Hoping to dwell in the house not made with hands.
In this, there is no end, only a new beginning.

AMBIENT

Each generation of leaves must pass,
As the wind shakes them to the ground;
When autumn comes, no leaf is spared,
No matter its beauty, no matter its ambience.

Ambient hum, ambient light,
Persistent through the night;
Orisons are sung by oracles,
Voices only to be muted in their might,
Ceaseless, then quietly ceasing—

On to be conjoined with other choirs.

FINIS

Made in the USA
Middletown, DE
08 July 2024

56980136R00106